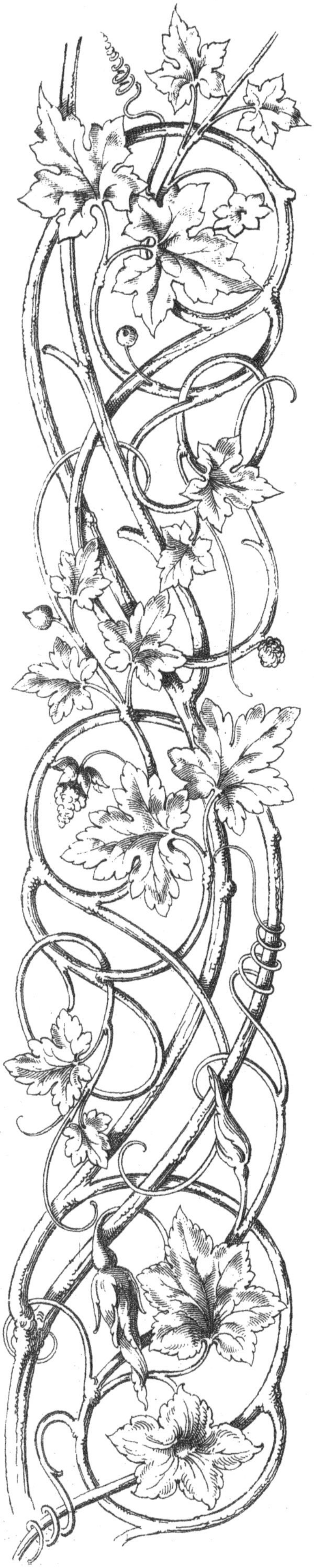

Fantastic Ornament

110 Designs and Motifs

Michel Liénard

Dover Publications
Garden City, New York

Copyright

Copyright © 2006 by Dover Publications
All rights reserved.

Bibliographical Note

This Dover edition, first published in 2006, is a new selection of 62 plates from *Liénard's Specimens of Decoration and Ornamentation,* originally published by J. O'Kane, New York, n.d.

DOVER *Pictorial Archive* SERIES

This book belongs to the Dover Pictorial Archive Series. You may use the designs and illustrations for graphics and crafts applications, free and without special permission, provided that you include no more than ten in the same publication or project. For permission for additional use, please email the Permissions Department at: rights@doverpublications.com or write to: Dover Publications, 1325 Franklin Ave, Suite 250, Garden City, NY 11530.

However, resale, licensing, republication, reproduction or distribution of any illustration by any other graphic service, whether it be in a book or in any other design resource, is strictly prohibited.

Library of Congress Cataloging-in-Publication Data

Liénard, Michel.
[Liénard's specimens of decoration and ornamentation. Selections]
Fantastic ornament : 110 designs and motifs / Michel Liénard.
p. cm.—(Dover pictorial archive series)
A new selection of plates from Liénard's specimens of decoration and ornamentation, originally published by J. O'Kane, New York.
ISBN 0-486-45229-8 (pbk.)
1. Decoration and ornament—Themes, motives. I. Title.

NK1535.L682 2006
745.4—dc22

2006048596

Printed in Canada
45229815 2025
www.doverpublications.com

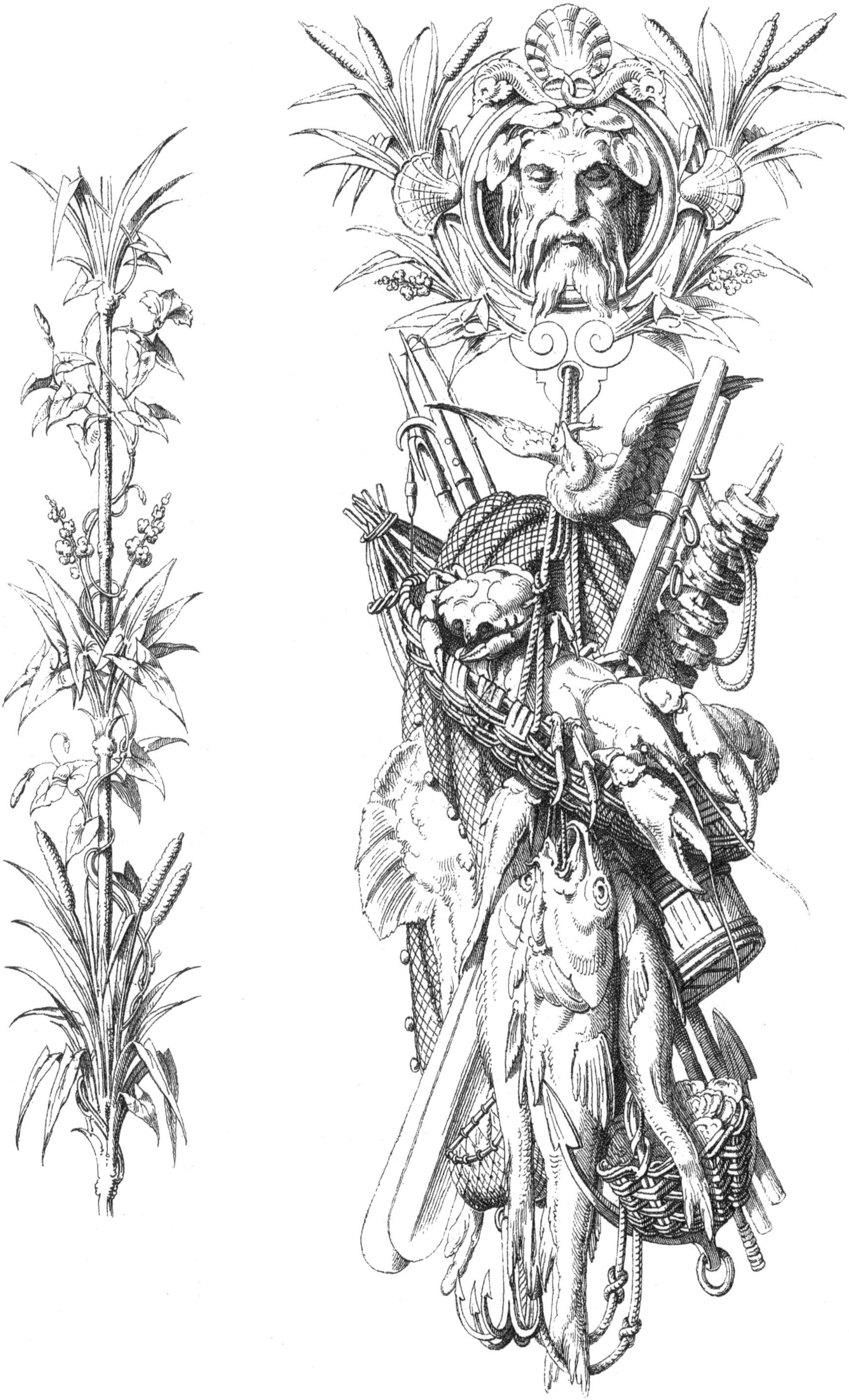

Fishing Trophy PLATE 1

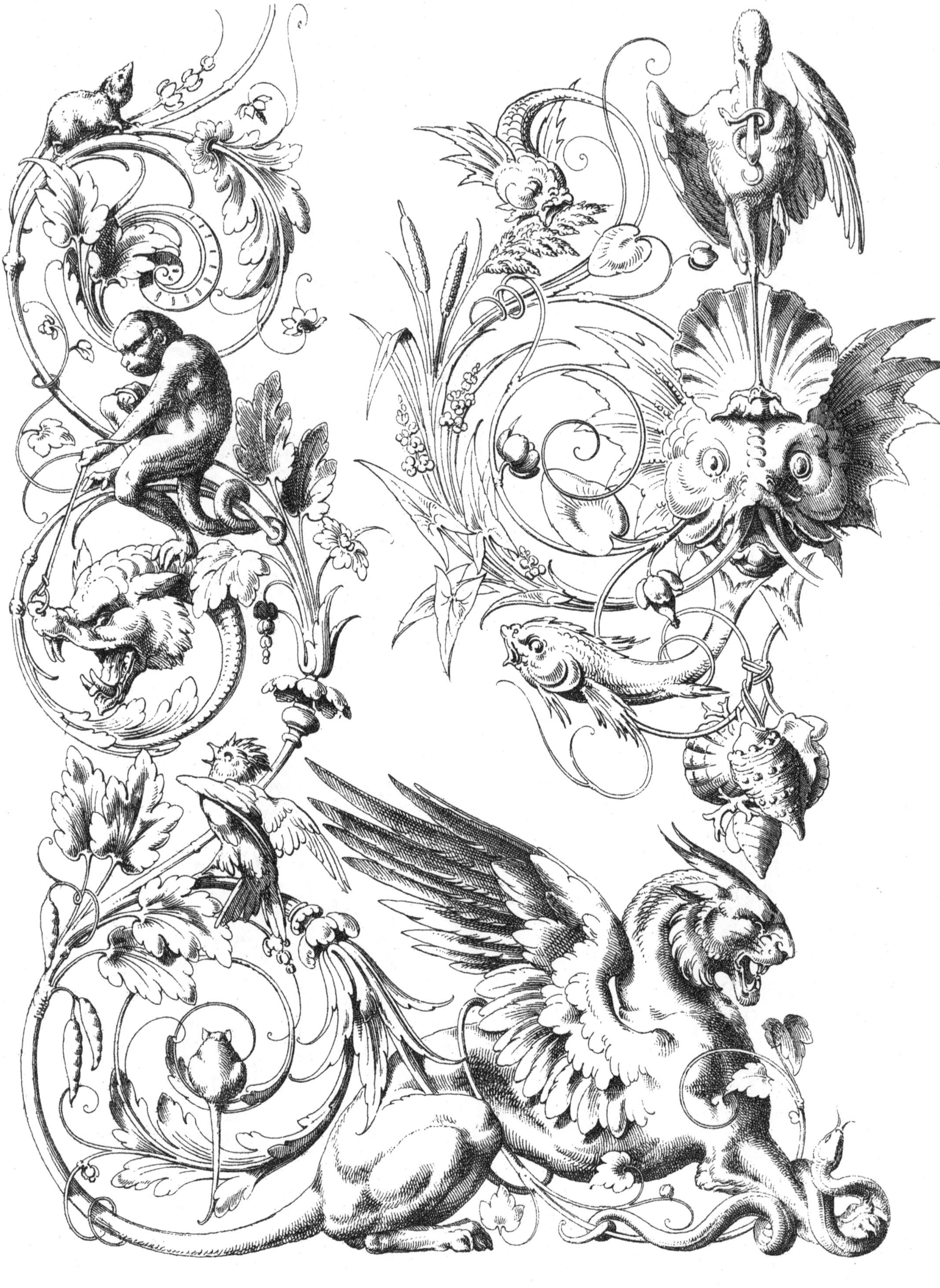

PLATE 2 *Aquatic Ornaments and Scrolls with Grotesques*

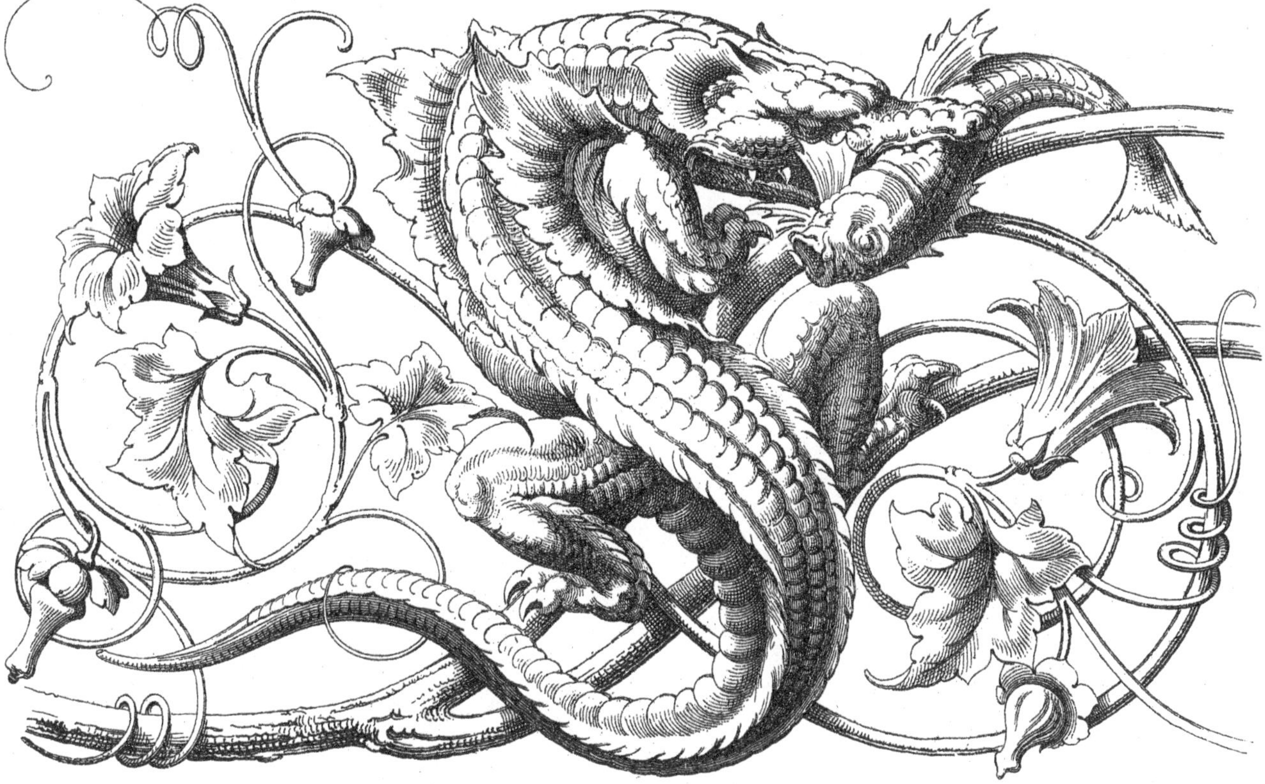

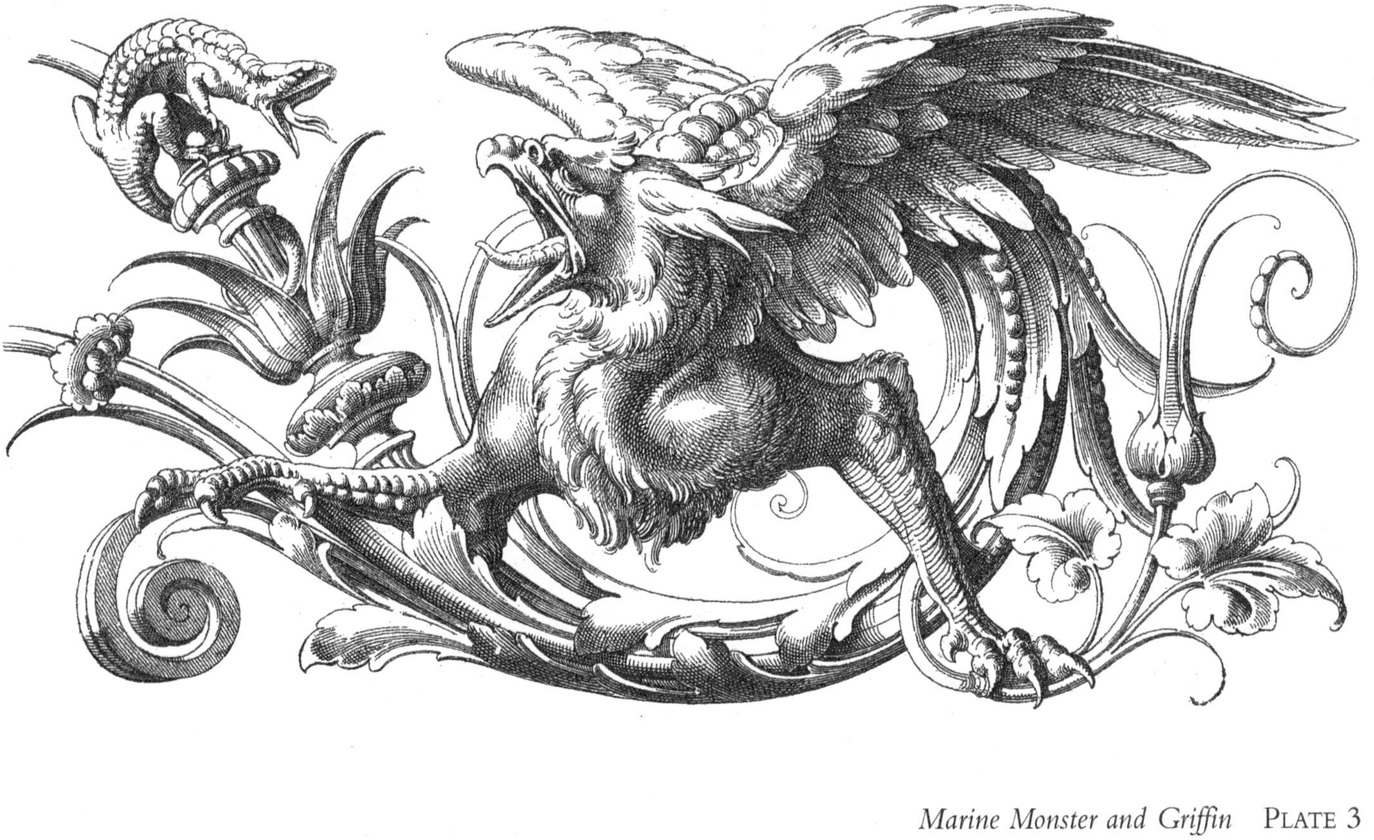

Marine Monster and Griffin PLATE 3

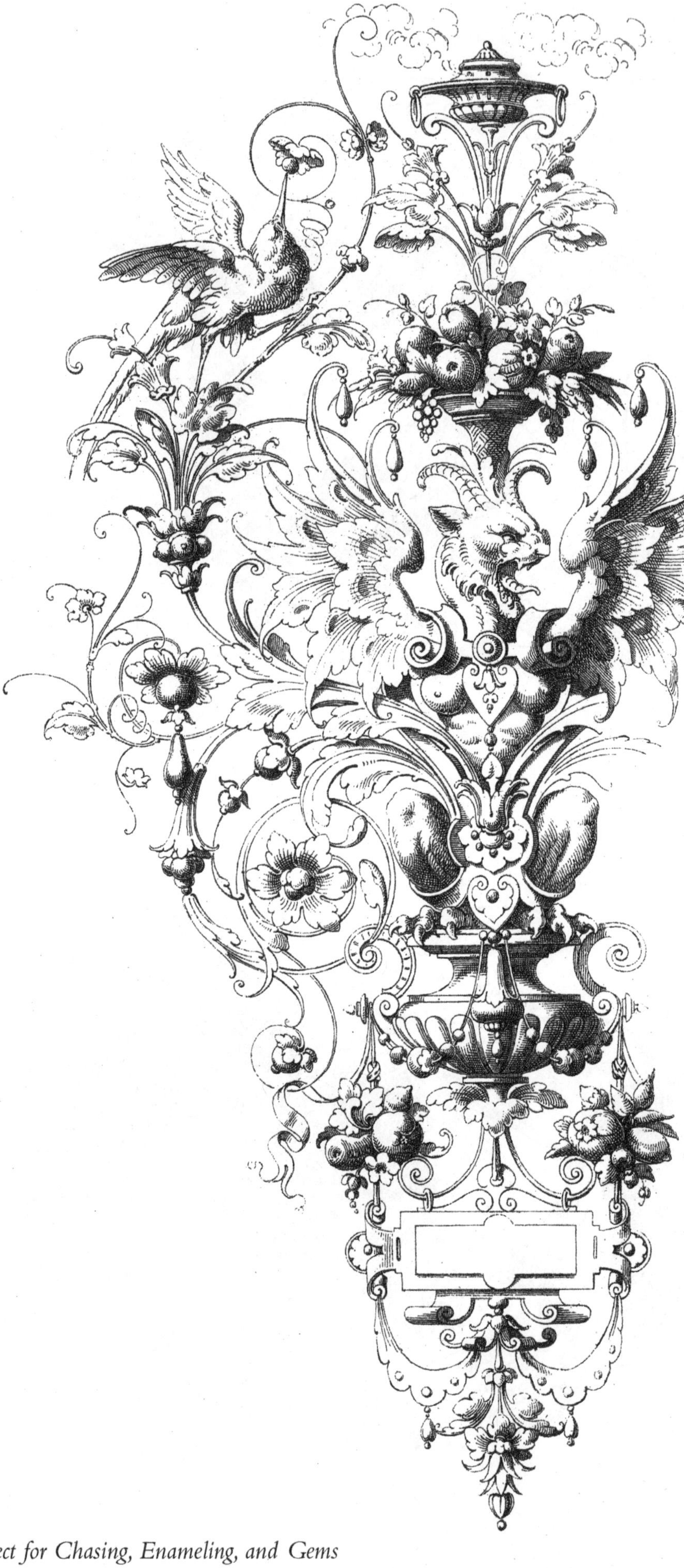

PLATE 4 *Subject for Chasing, Enameling, and Gems*

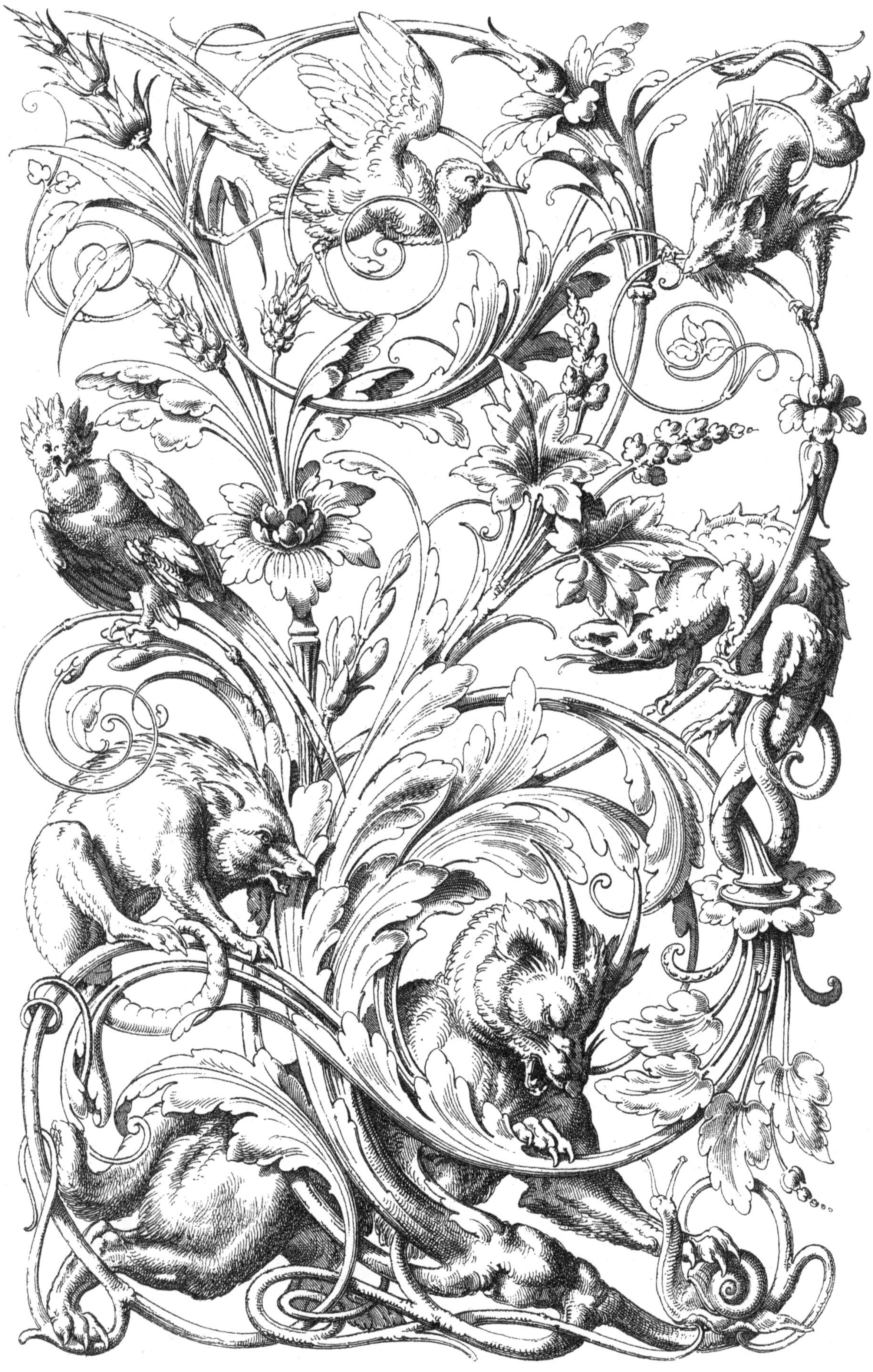

Scrolls with Grotesque Animals PLATE 5

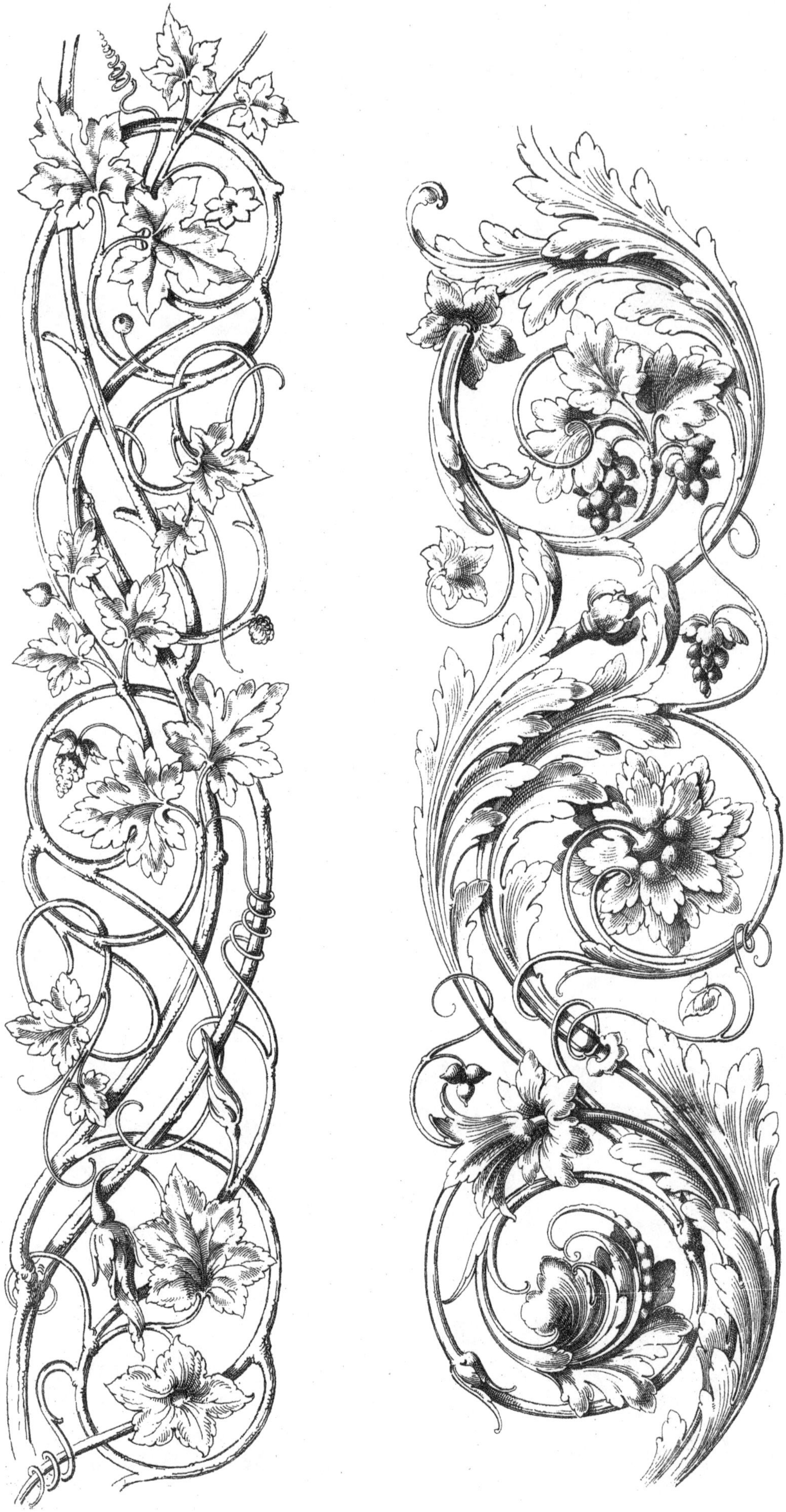

PLATE 6 *Running Ornaments of Natural Foliage*

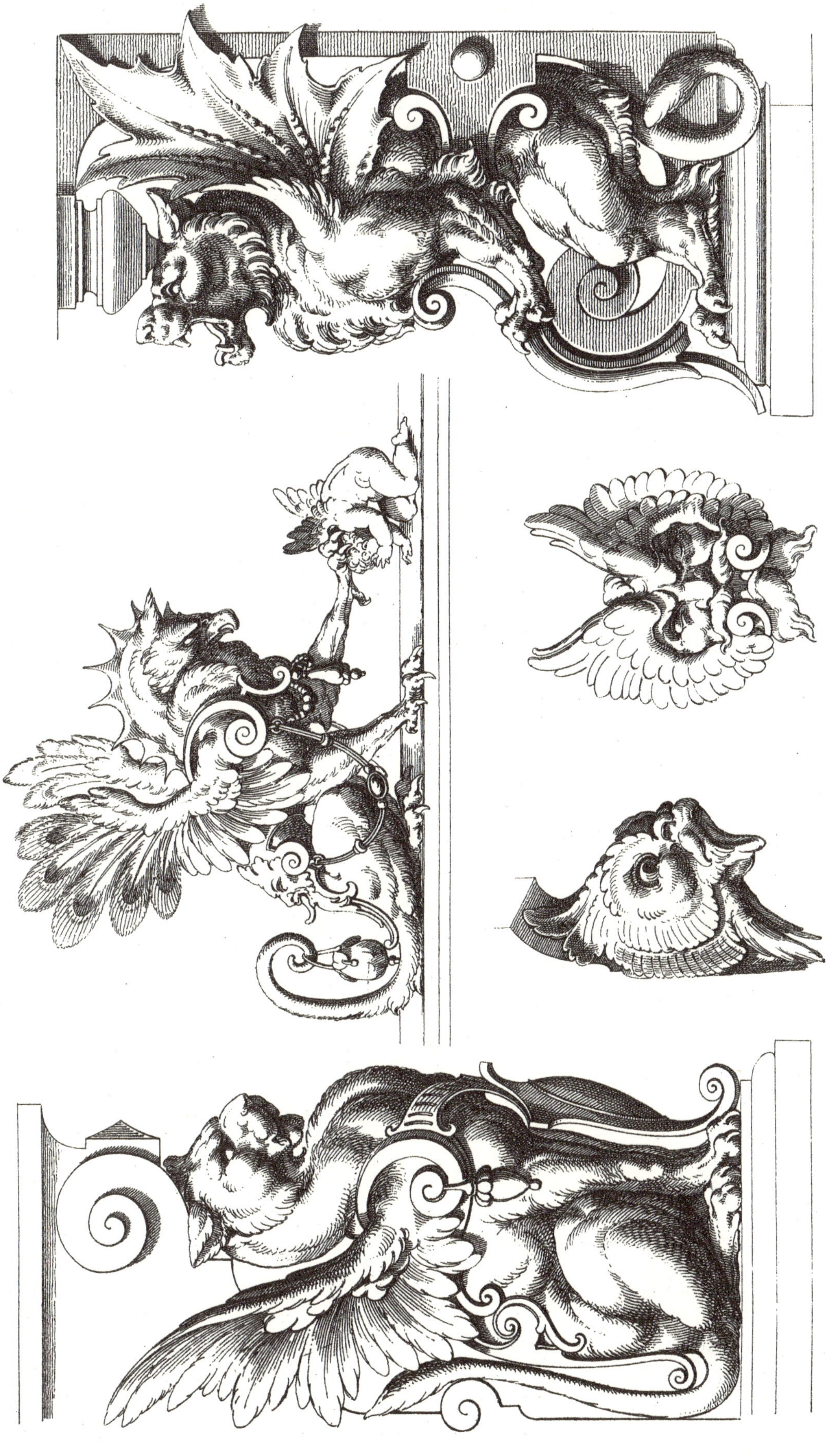

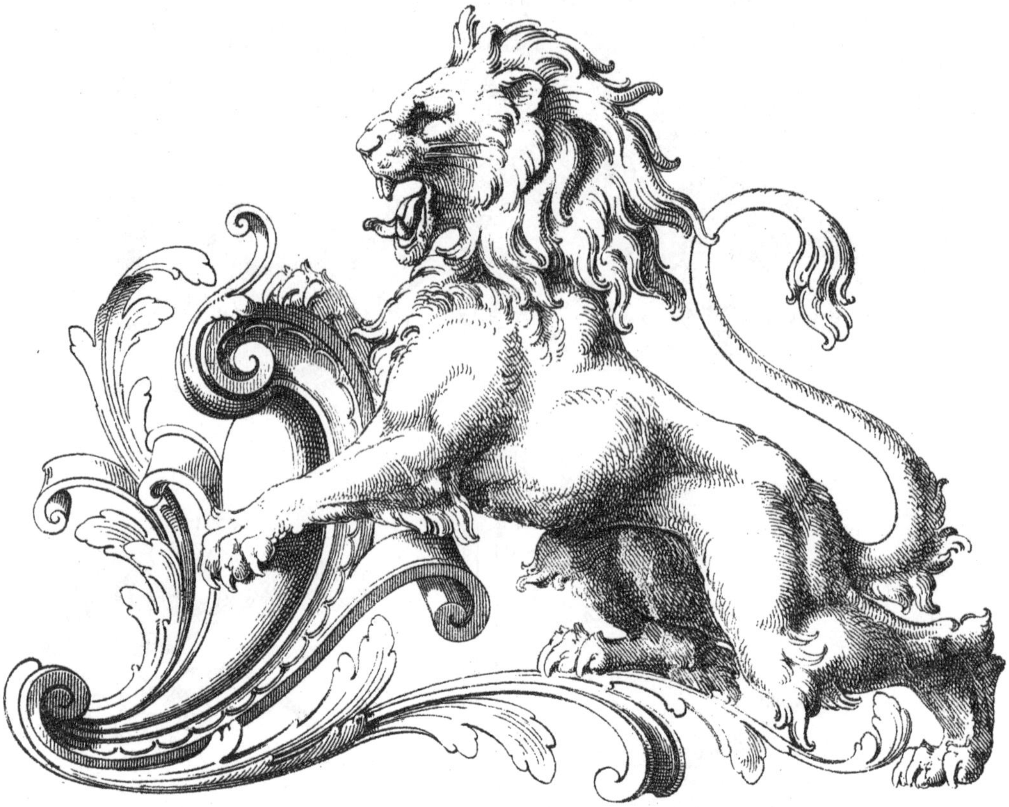

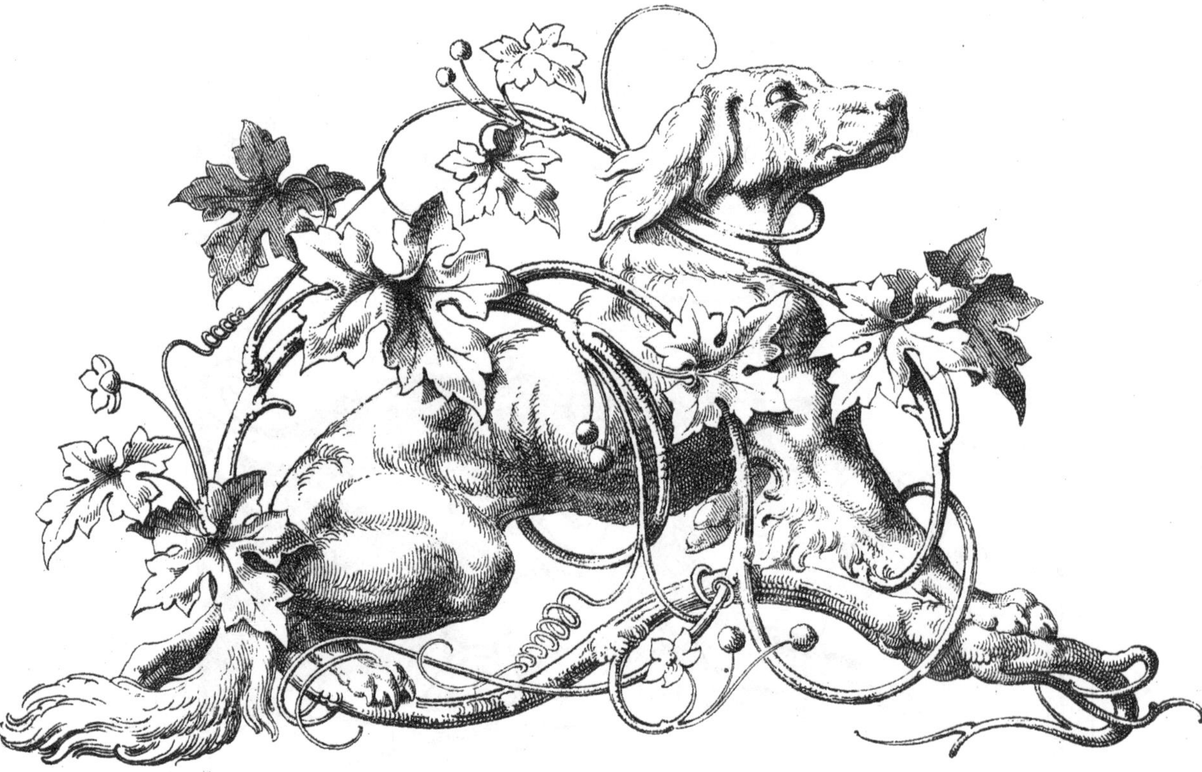

PLATE 8 *Heraldic Lion and Hunting Subject*

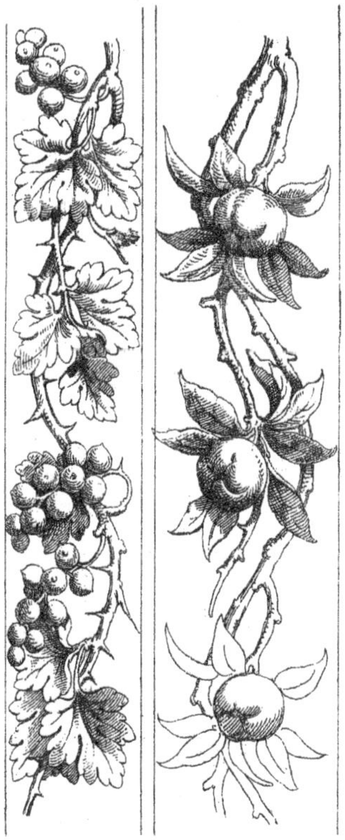

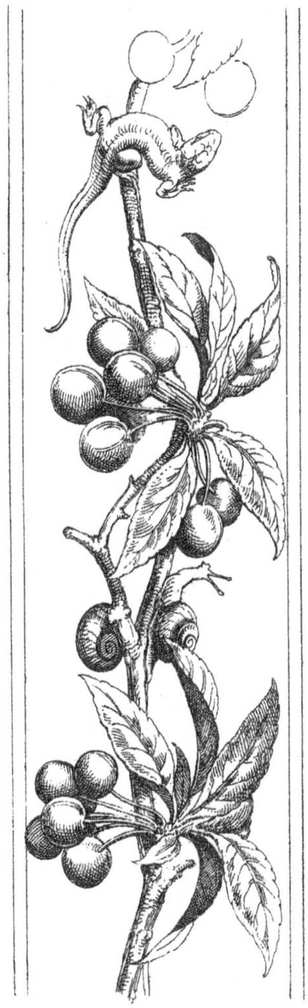

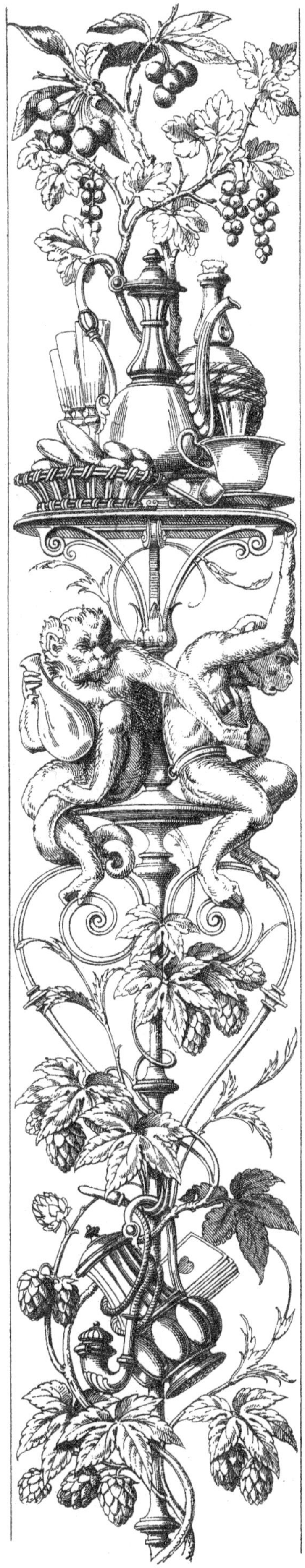

Naturalistic Ornament and Decoration for an Inn PLATE 9

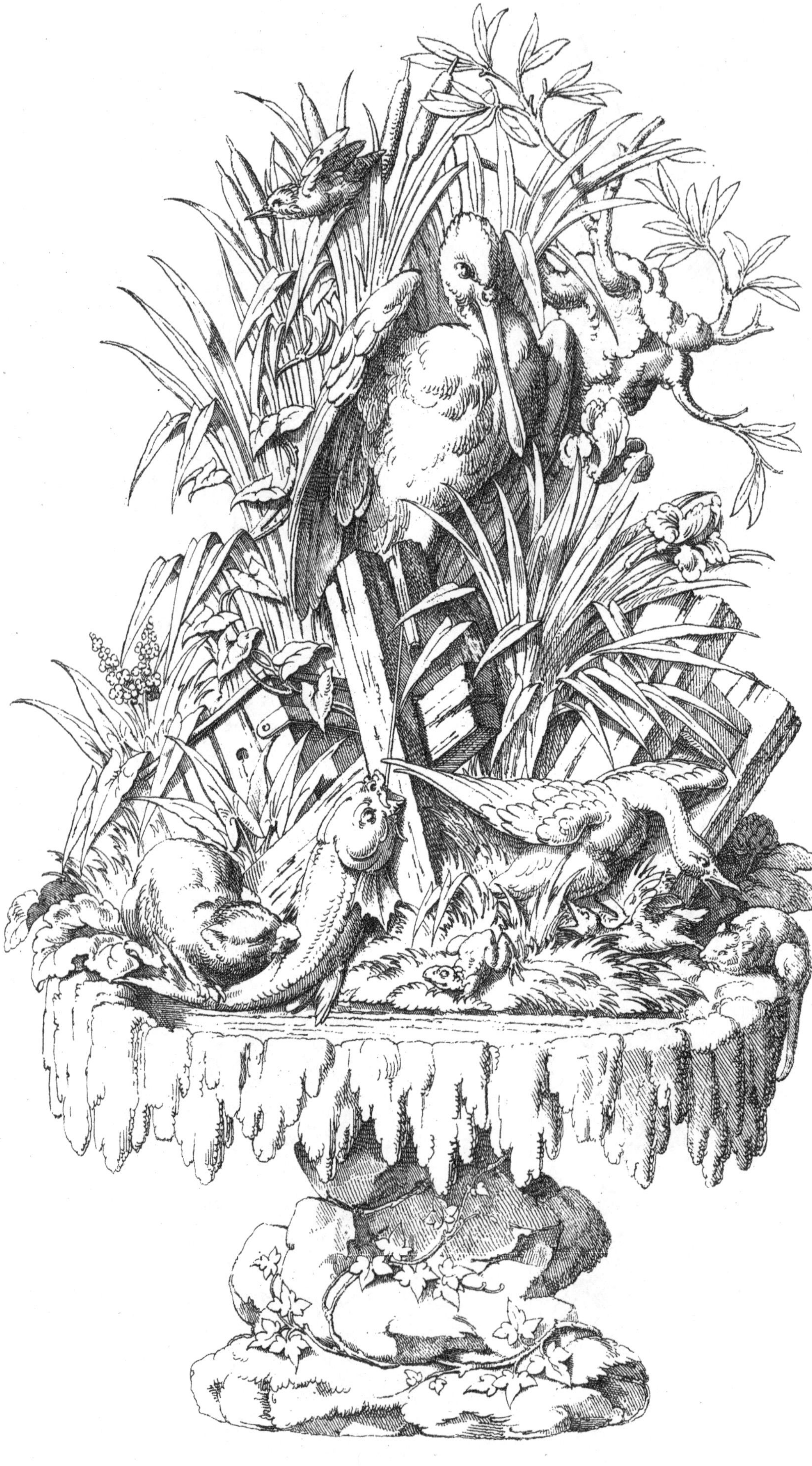

PLATE 10 *Fountain for Ceramics with Birds, Ornaments, and Fish*

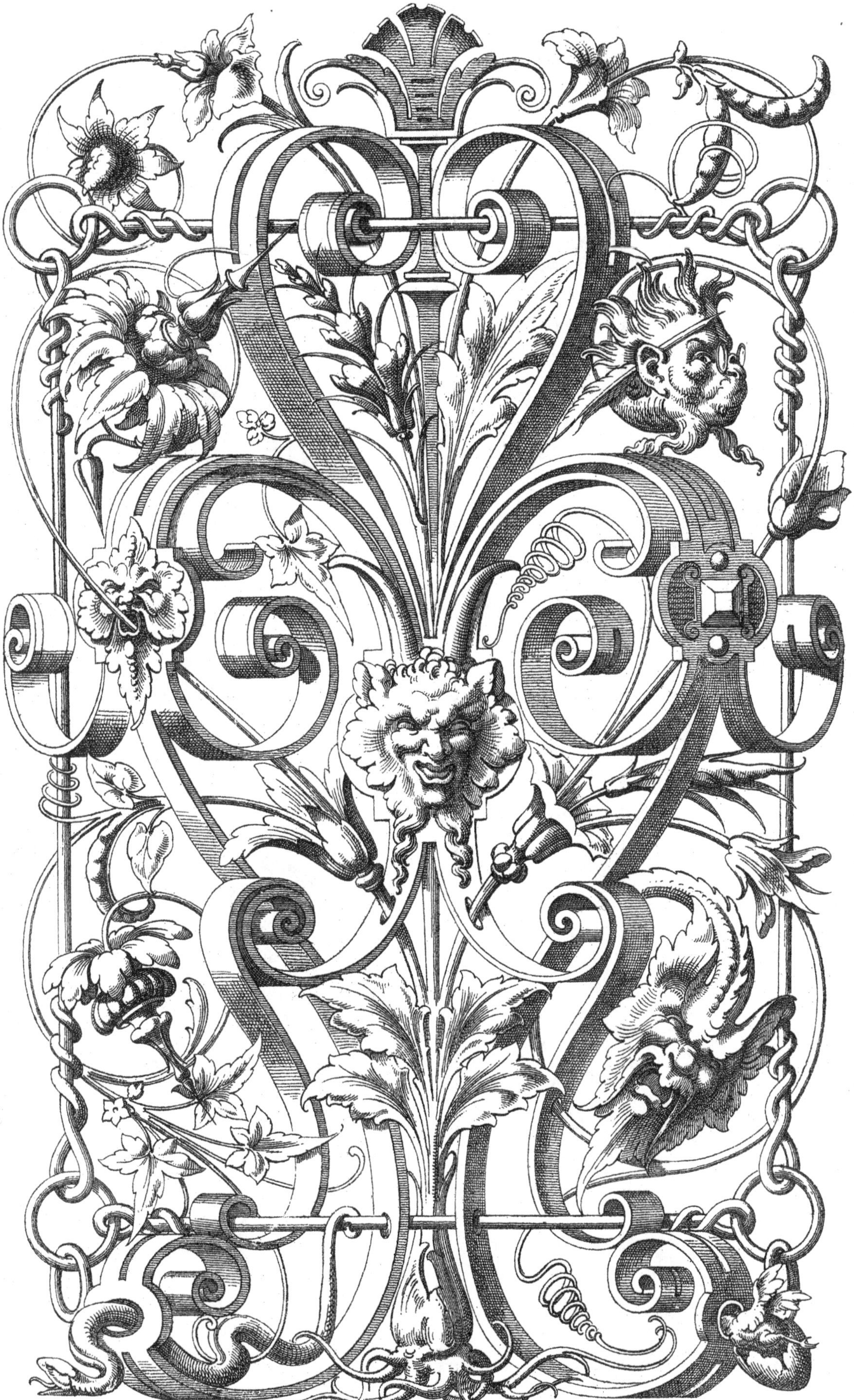

Decoration for a Panel PLATE 11

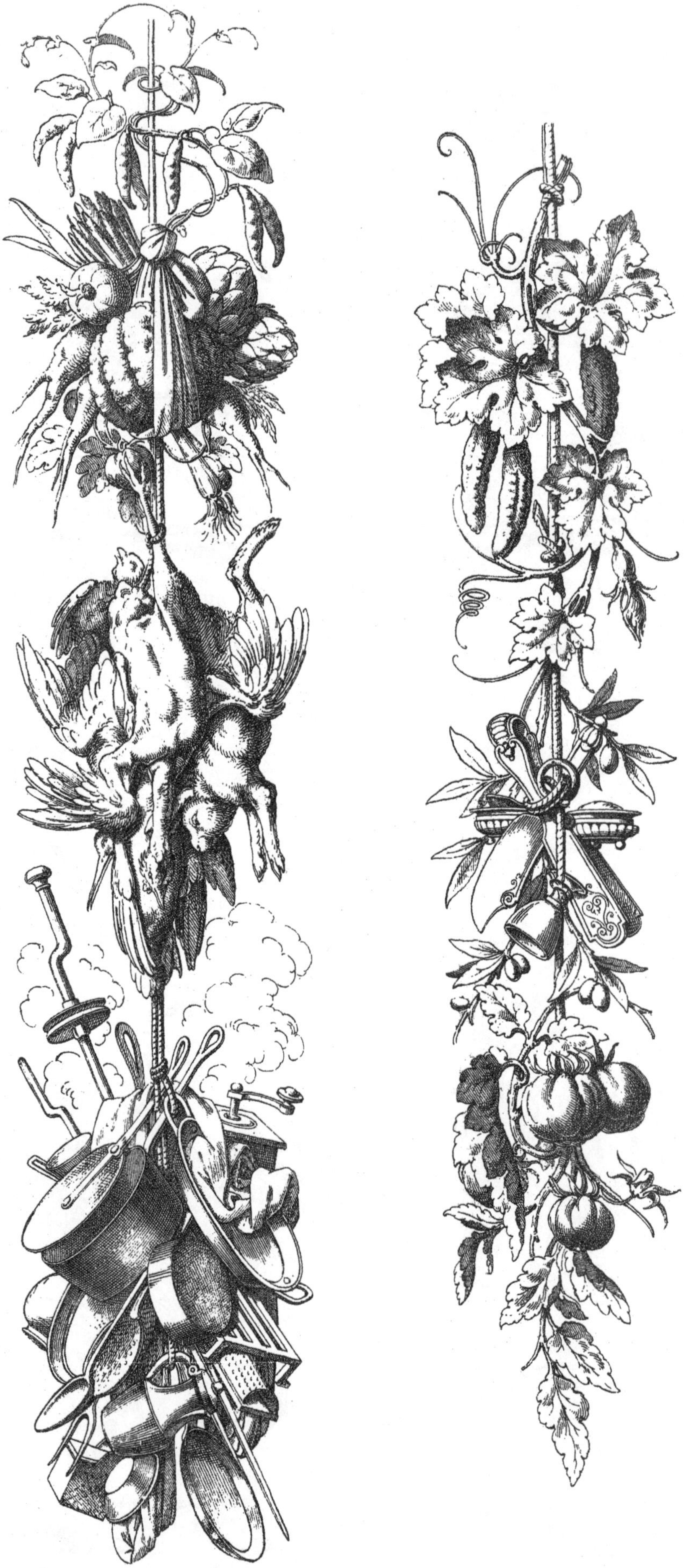

PLATE 12 *Trophies of Foliage, Game, and Culinary Objects*

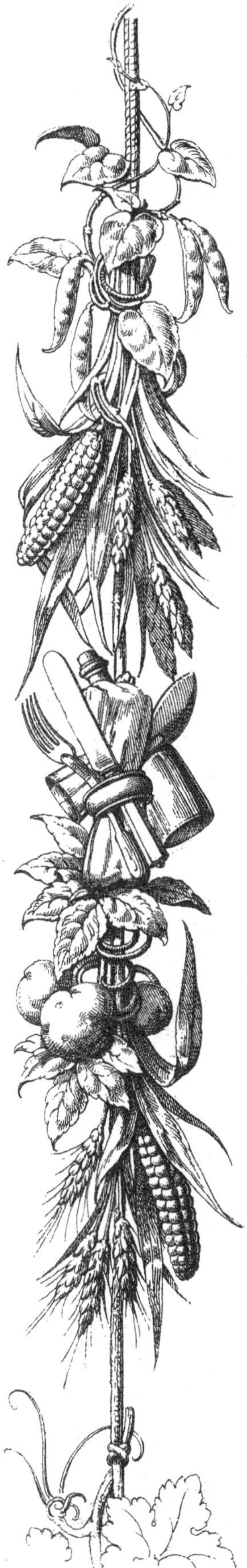

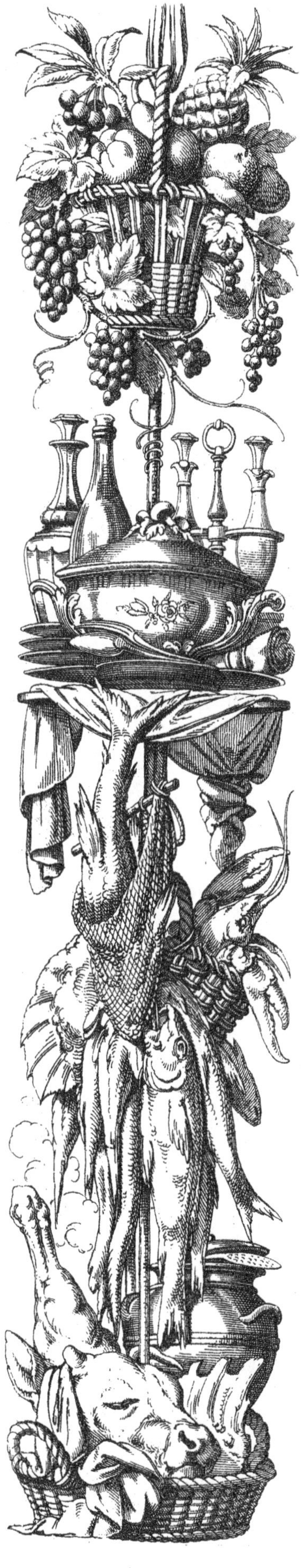

Trophies of Foliage, Game, and Culinary Objects PLATE 13

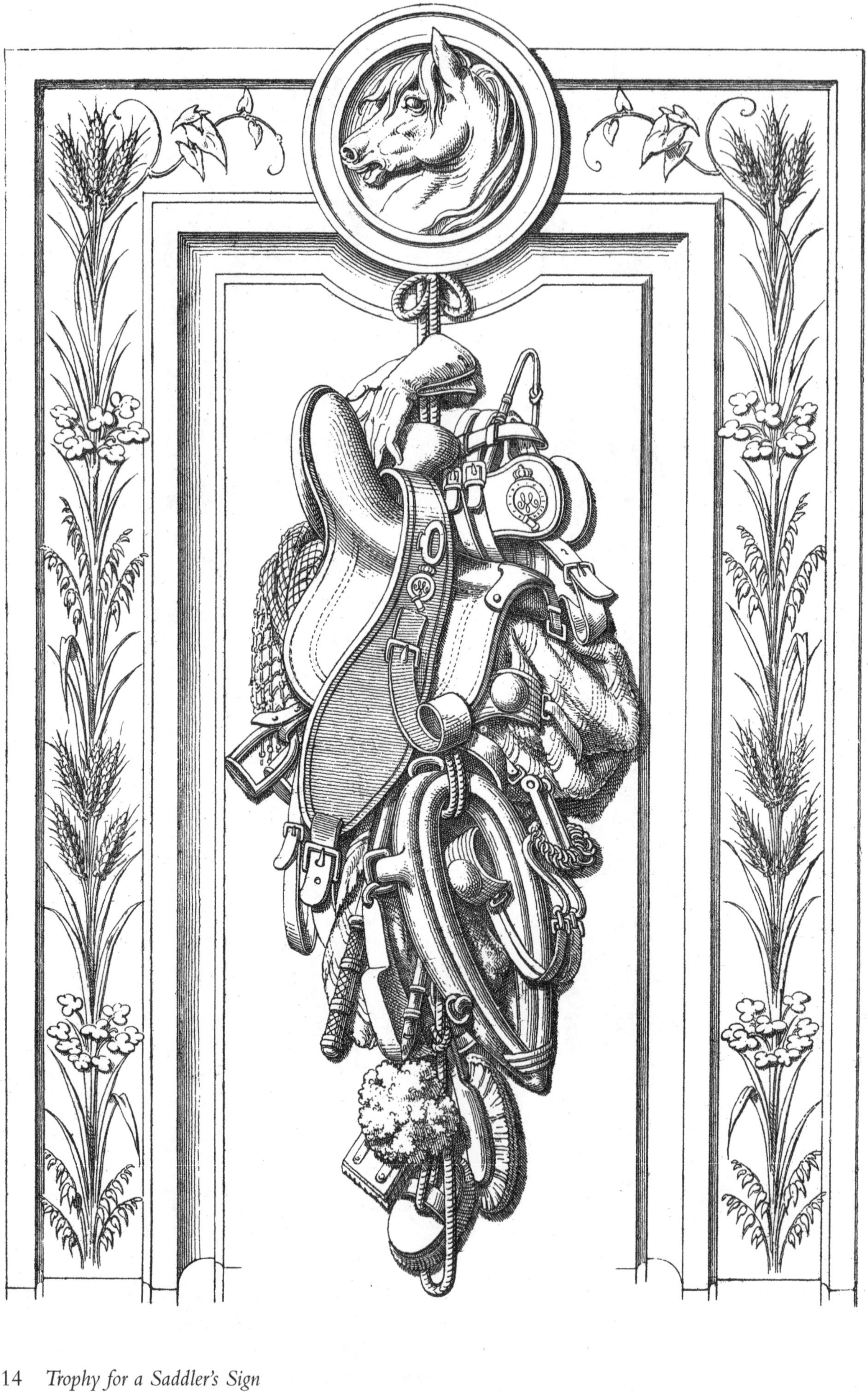

PLATE 14 *Trophy for a Saddler's Sign*

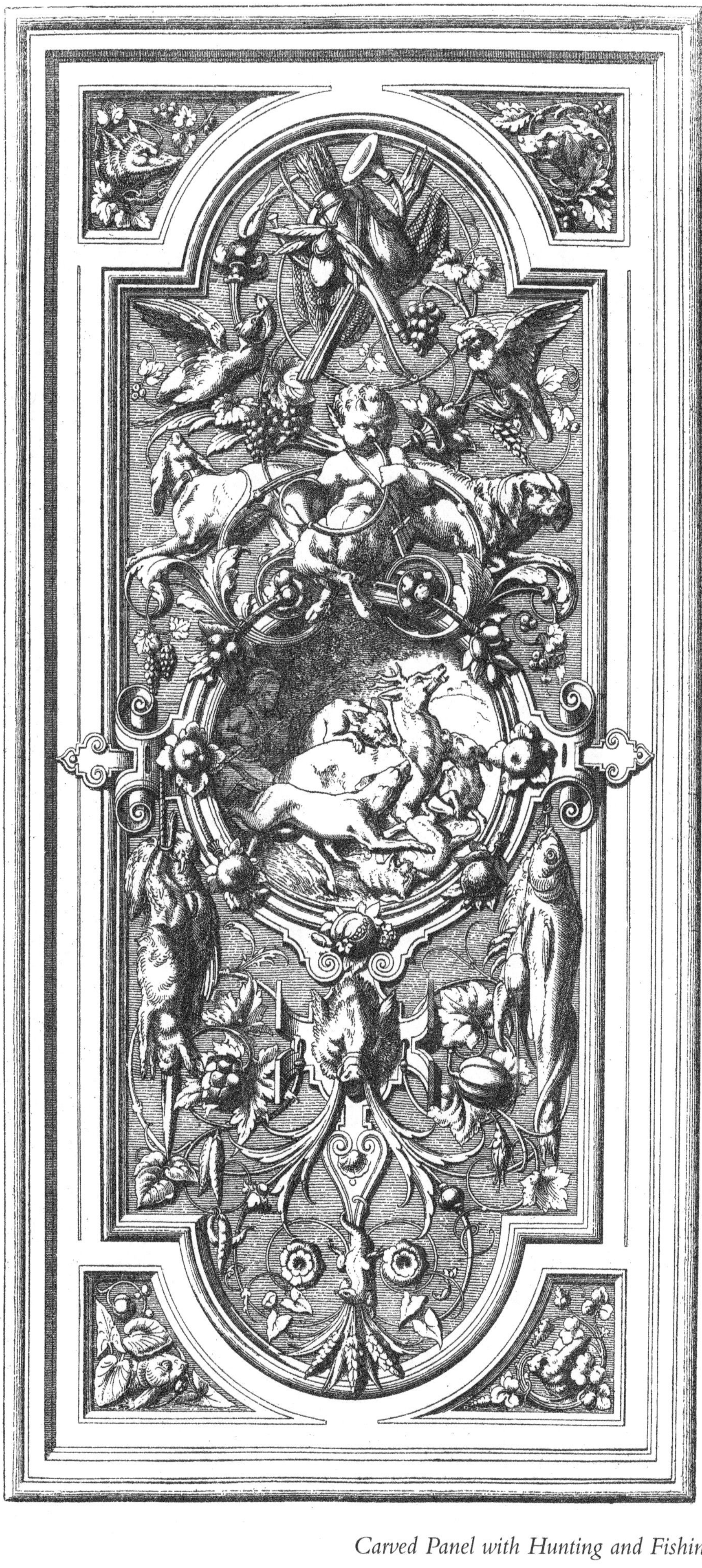

Carved Panel with Hunting and Fishing Details PLATE 15

PLATE 16 *Ornamental Caprice*

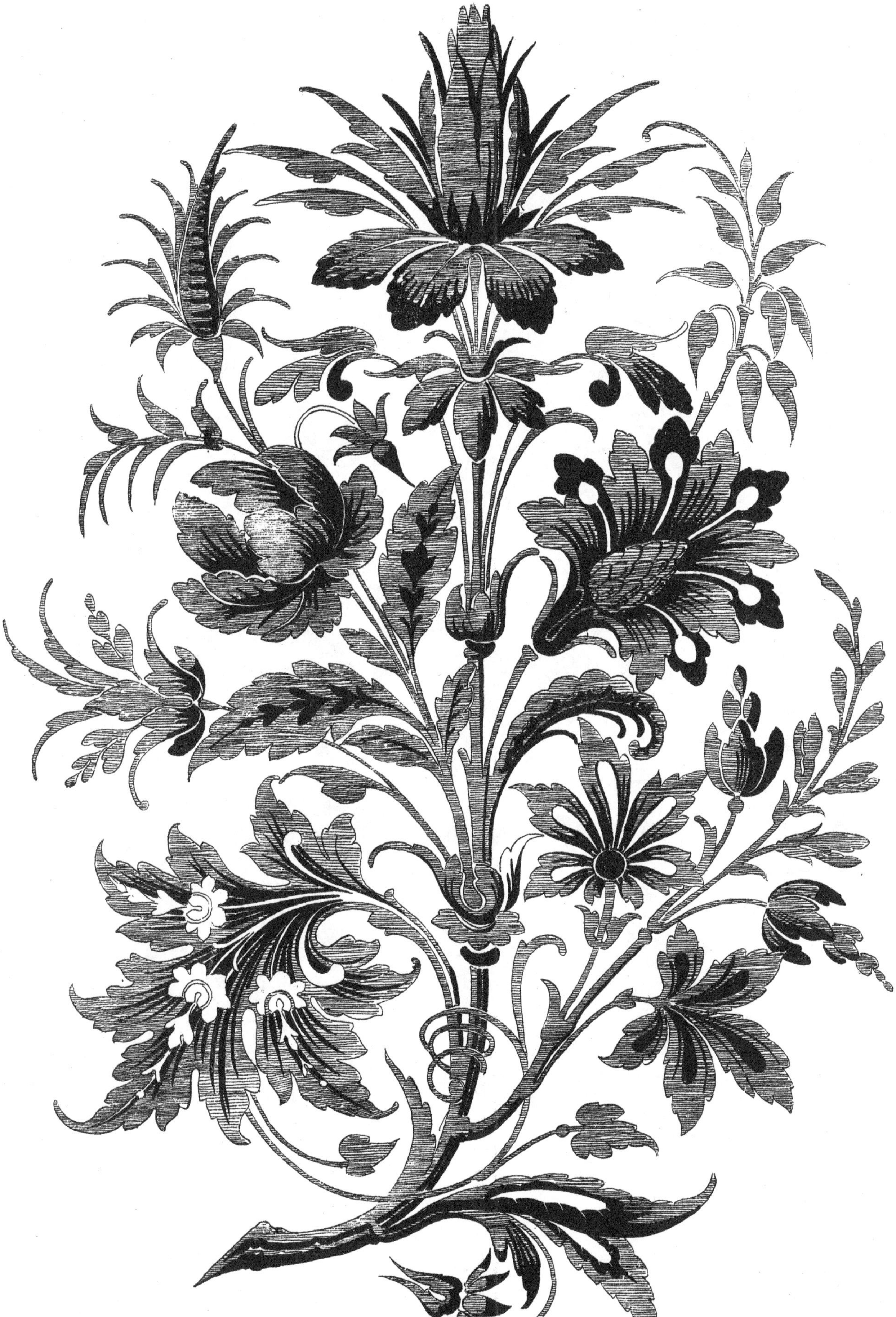

Floral Ornament PLATE 17

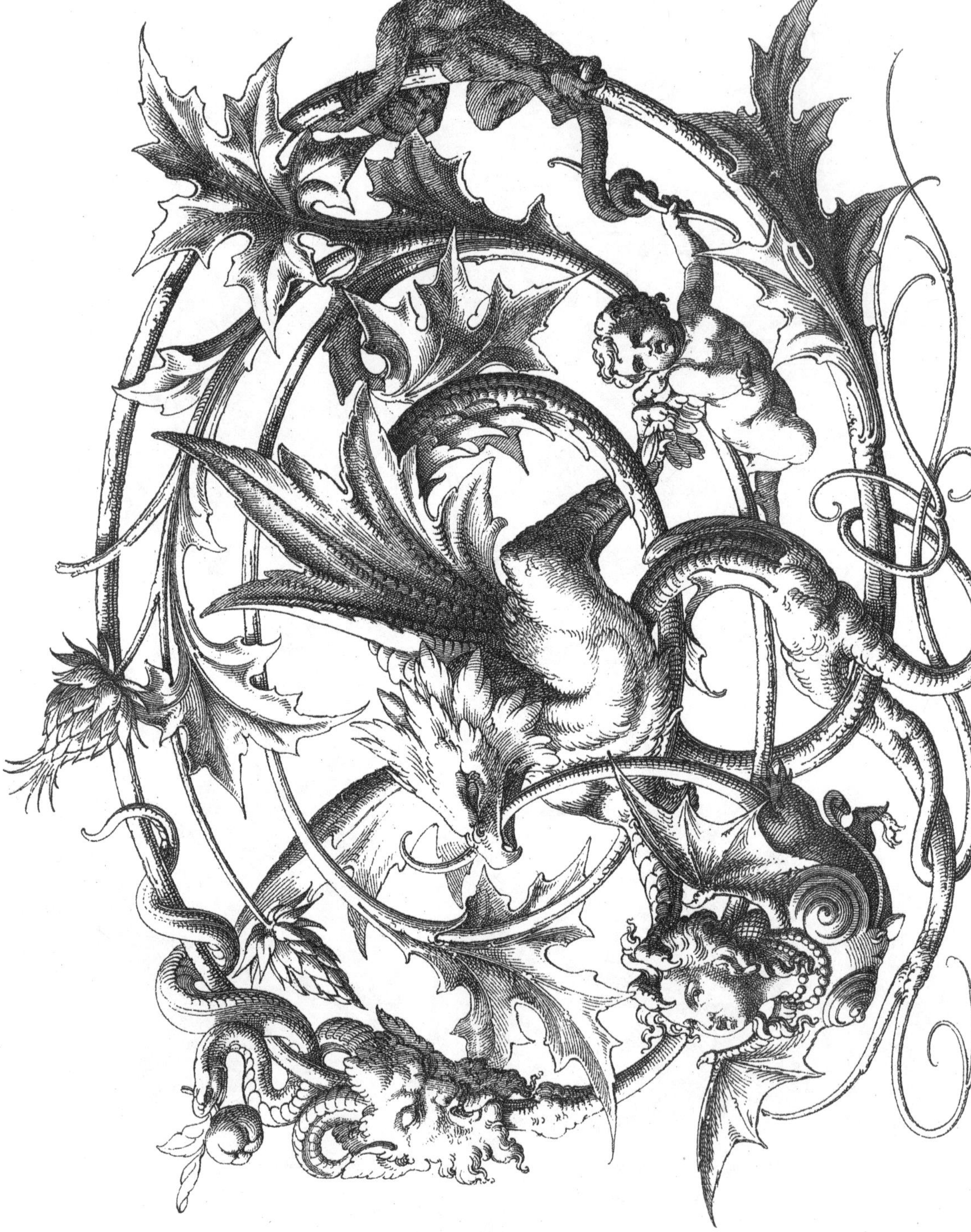

PLATE 18 *Grotesque Scroll*

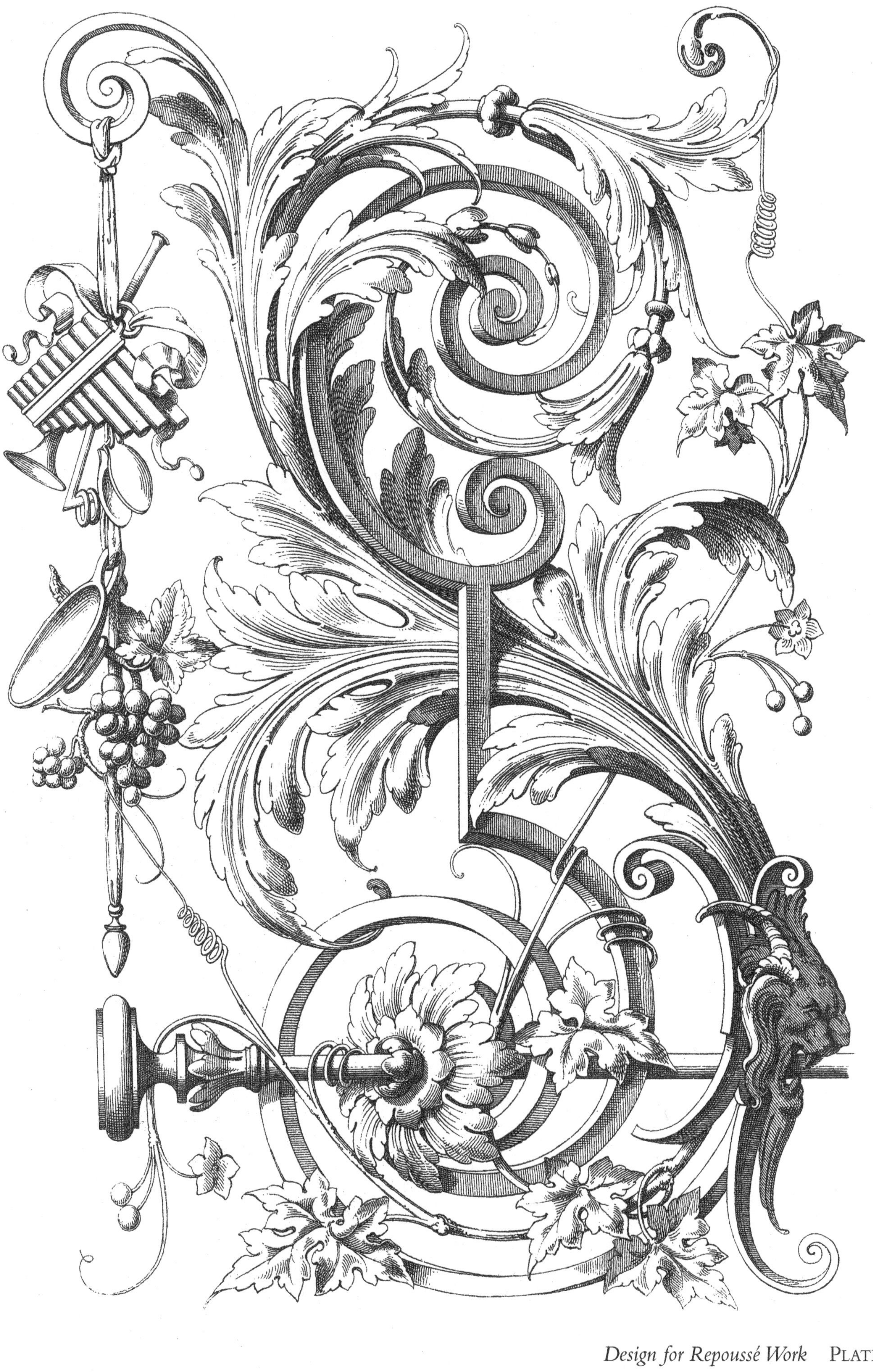

Design for Repoussé Work PLATE 19

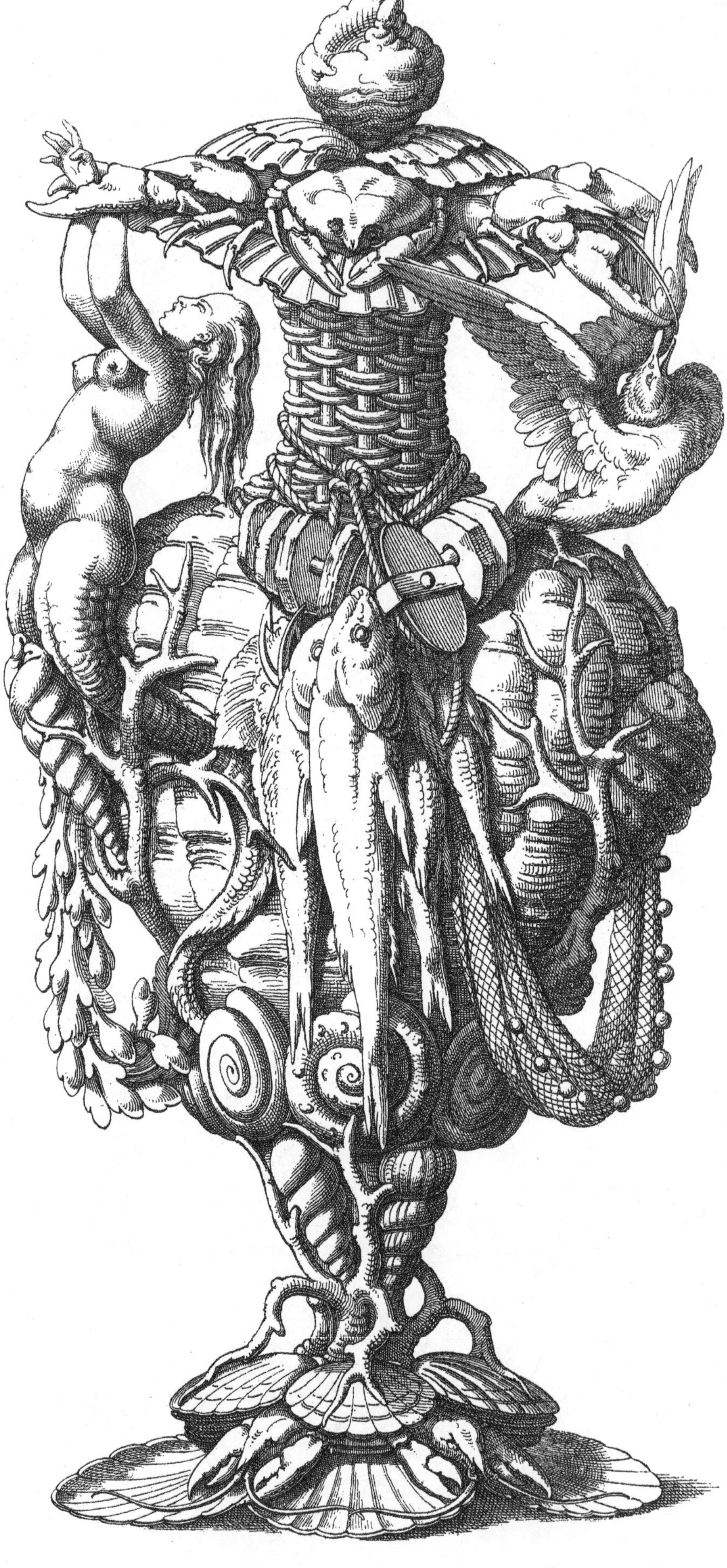

PLATE 20 *Enameled Terra Cotta Vase with Natural Ornaments*

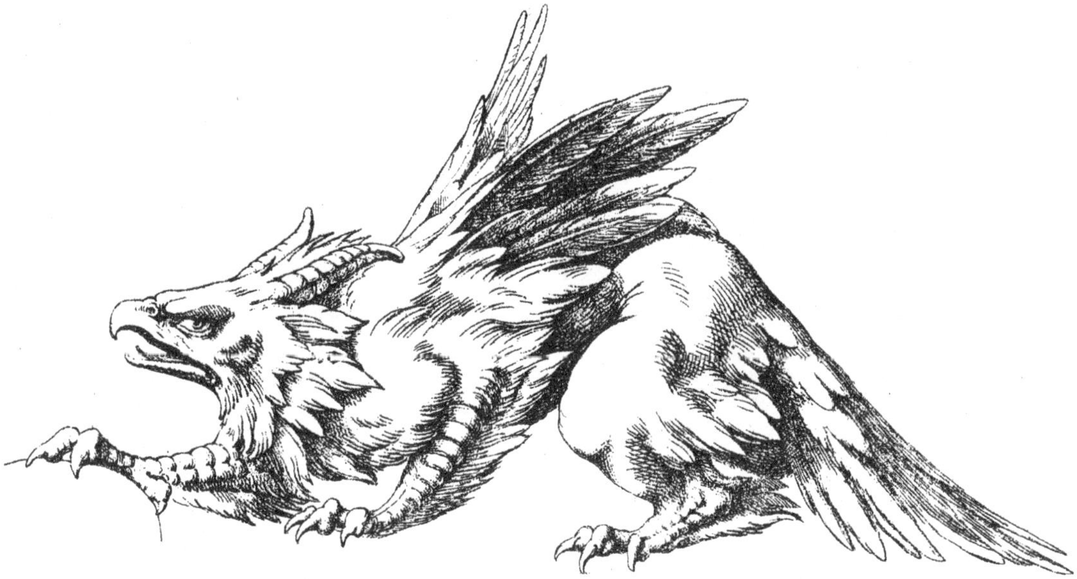

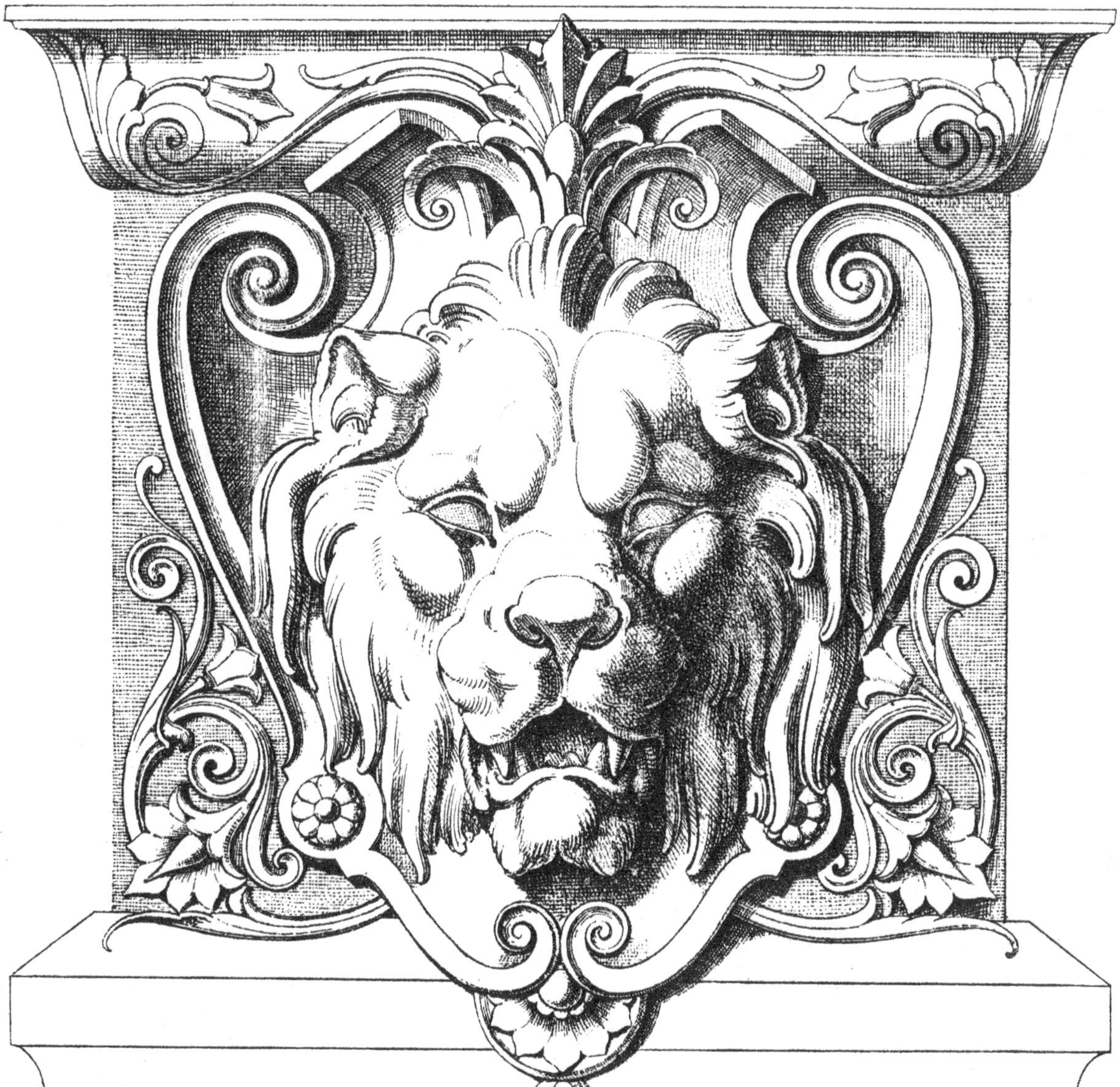

Mask and Griffin PLATE 21

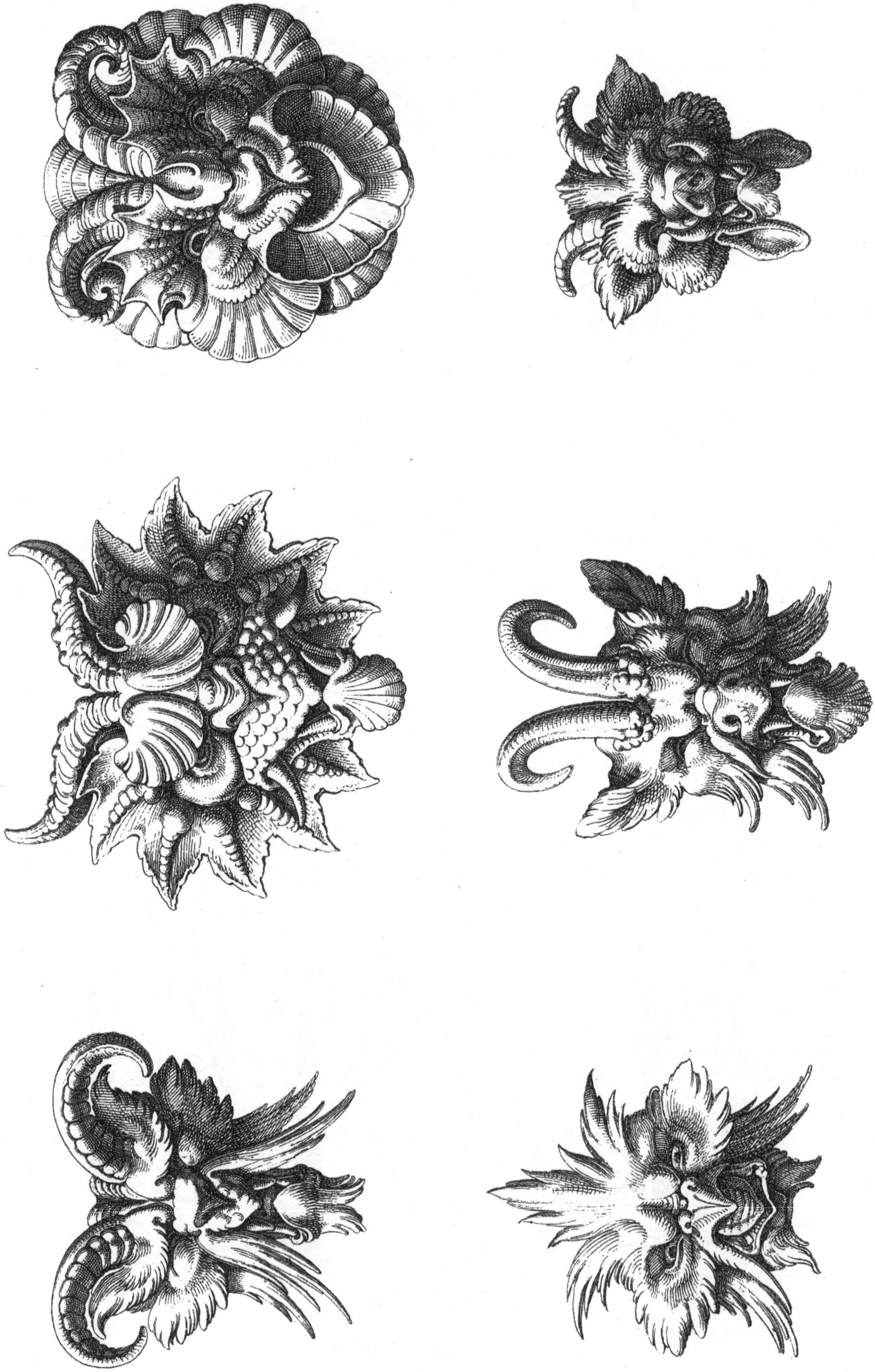

PLATE 22 *Grotesque Masks*

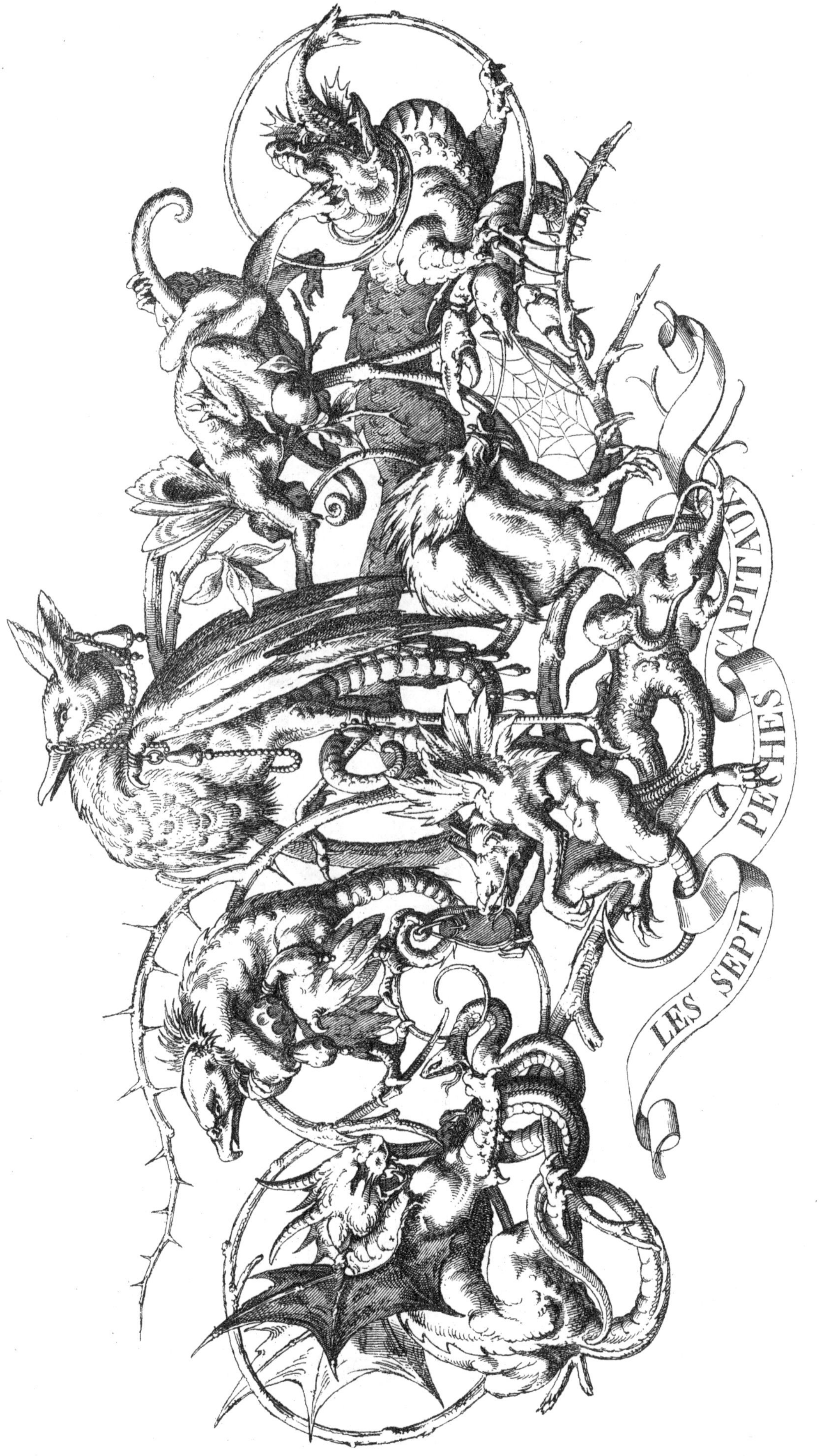
LES SEPT PECHES CAPITAUX

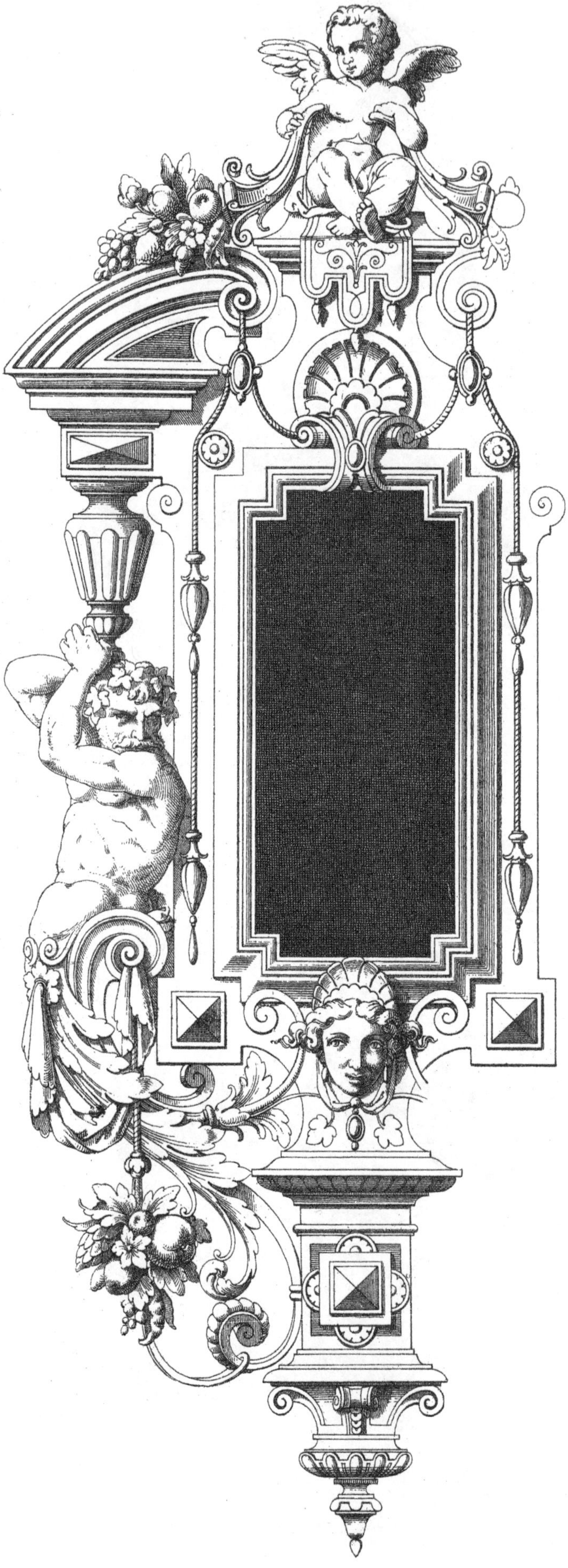

PLATE 24 *Cartouche Forming Frame*

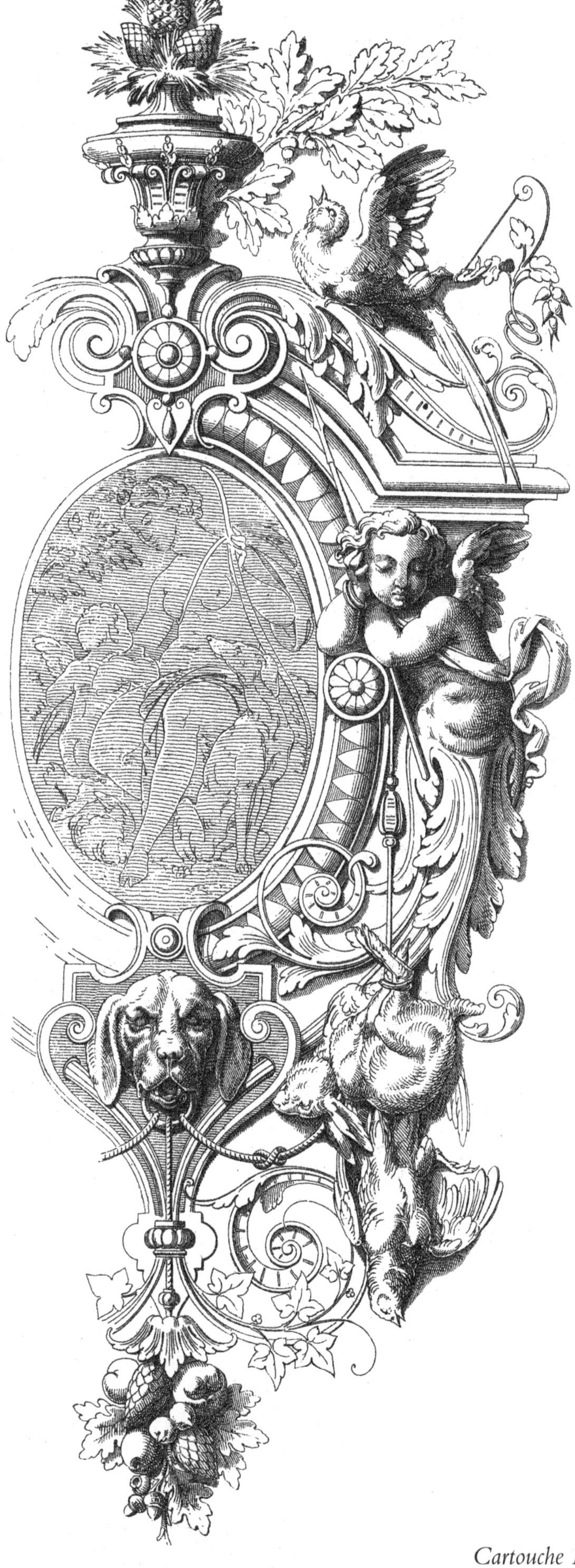

Cartouche Forming Frame PLATE 25

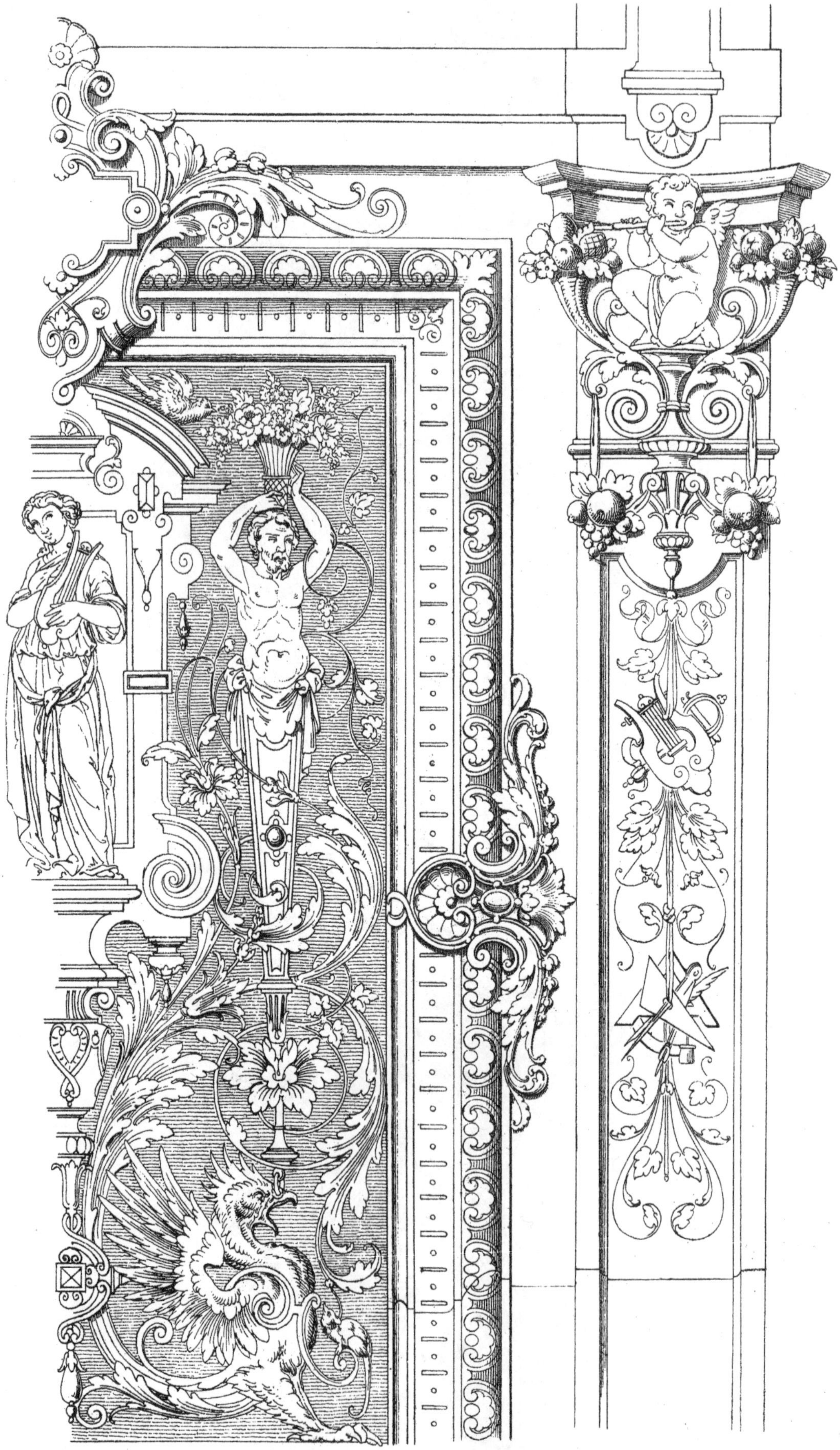

PLATE 26 *Panel for Painting or Tapestry, with Frame and Details*

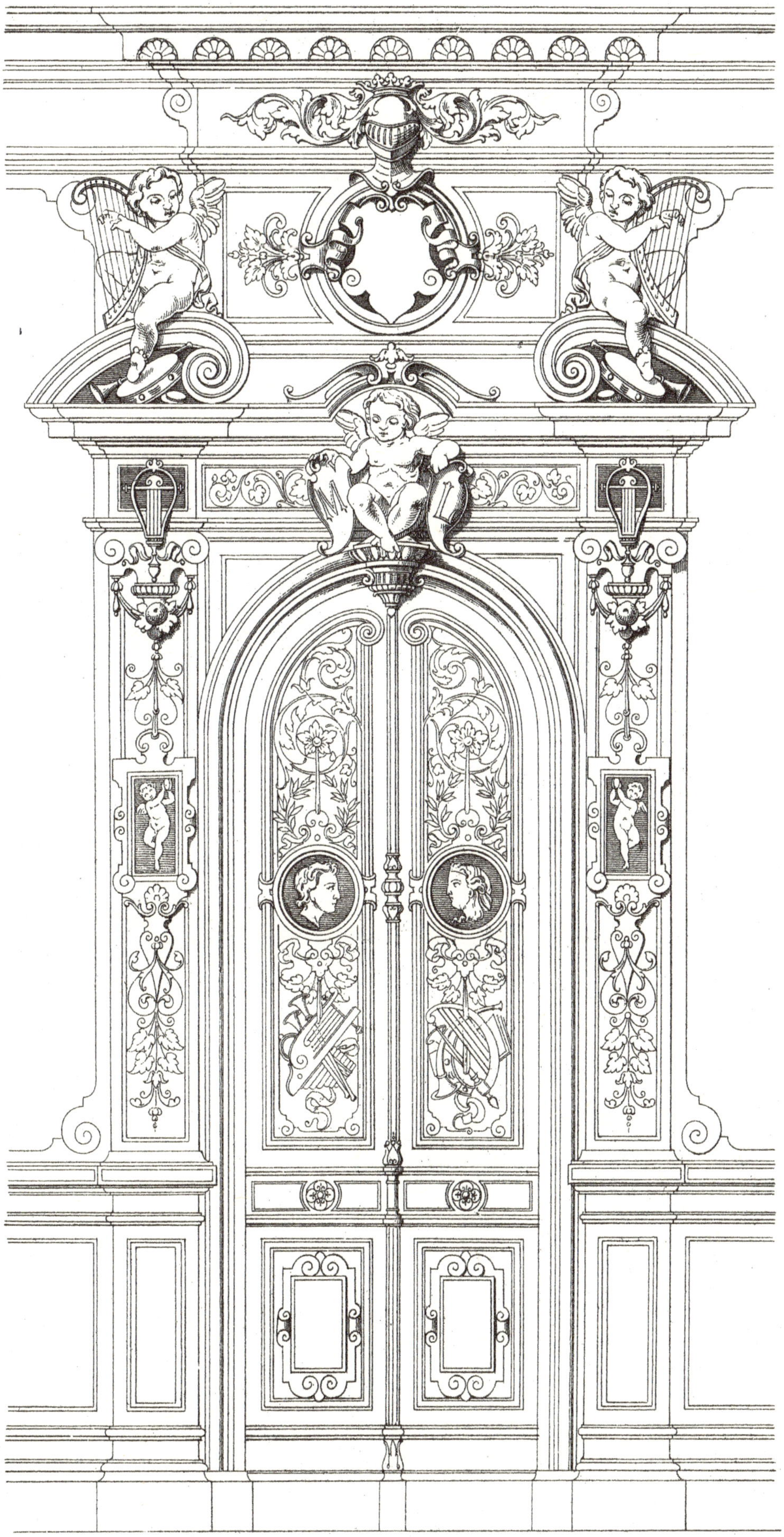

Drawing Room Door PLATE 27

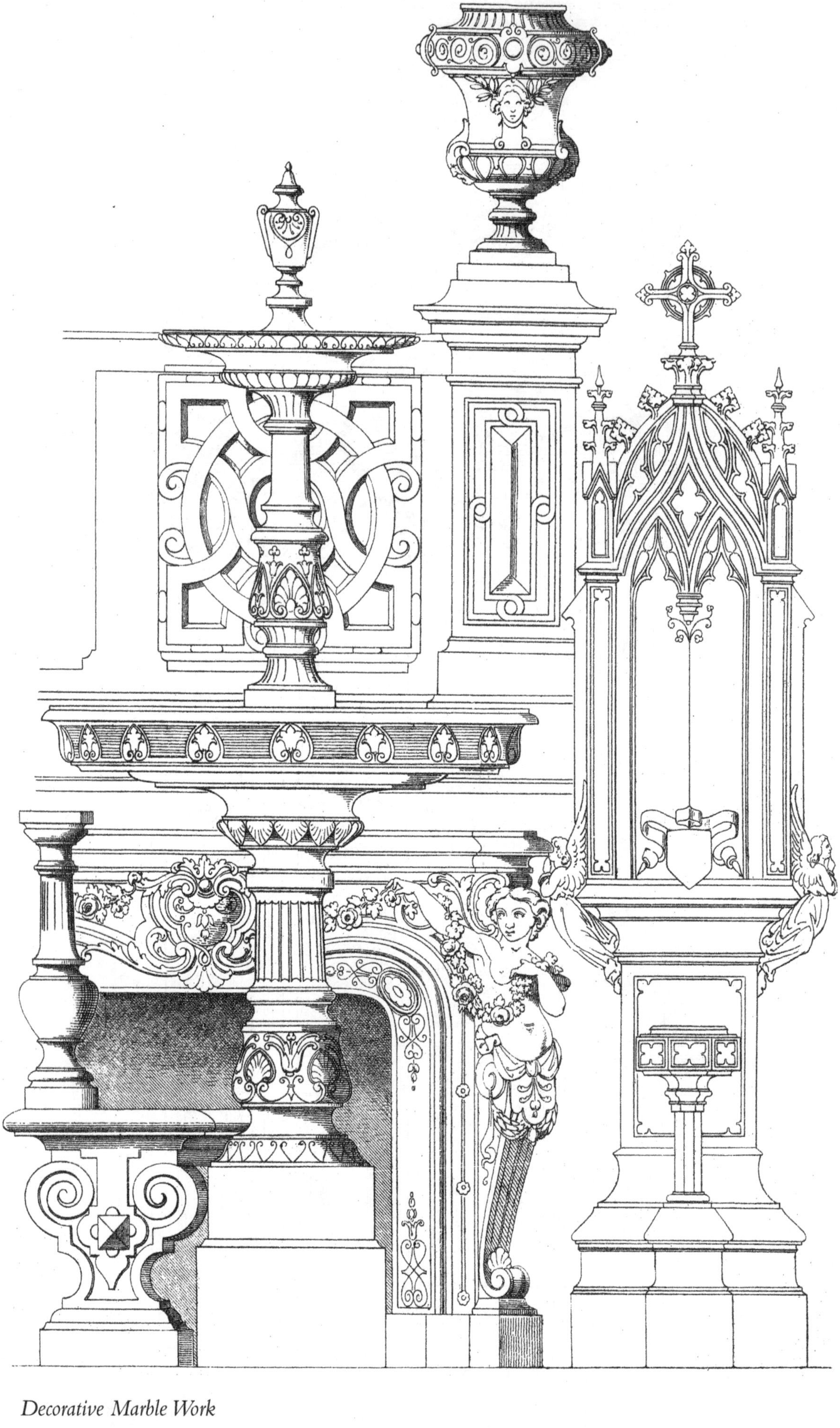

PLATE 28 *Decorative Marble Work*

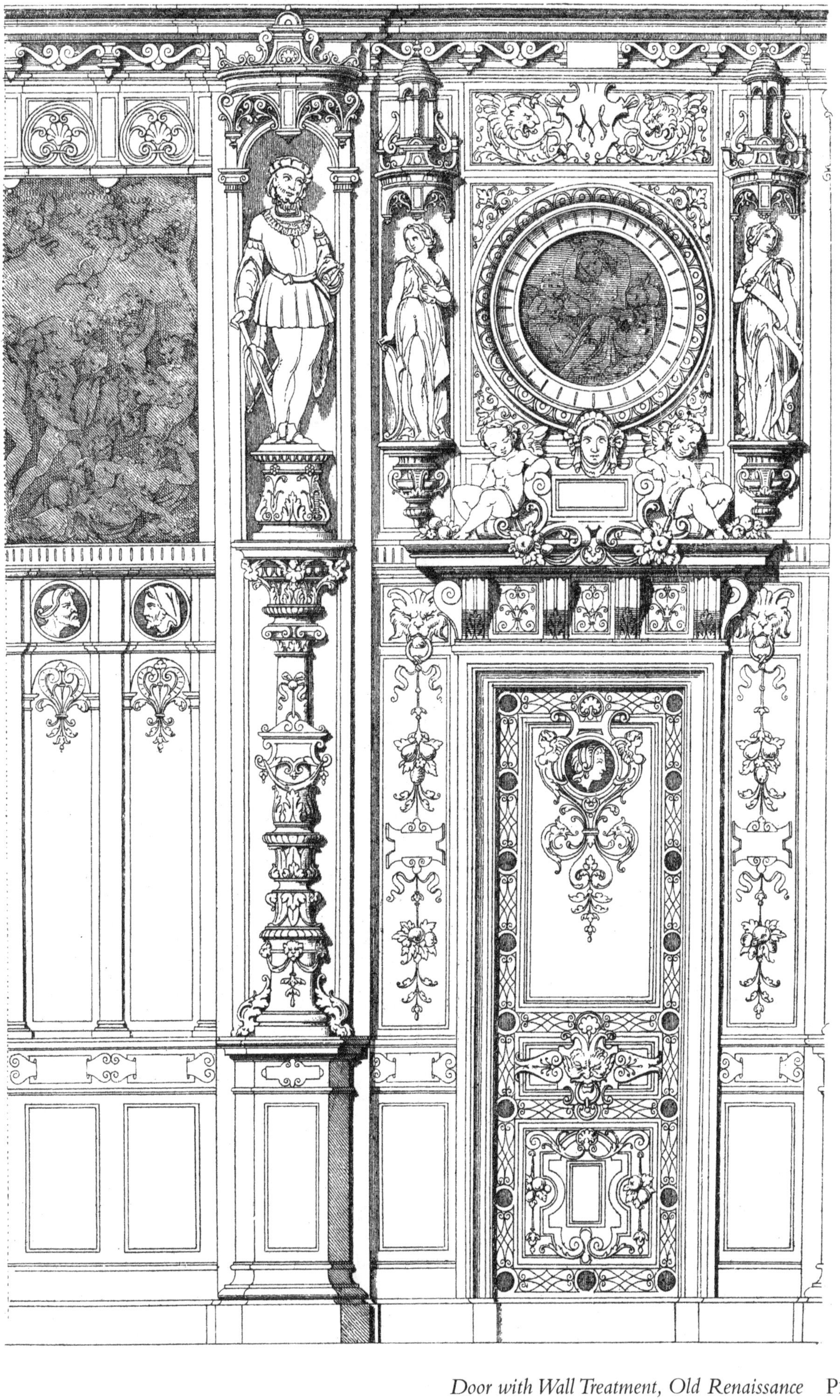

Door with Wall Treatment, Old Renaissance PLATE 29

PLATE 30 *Enlarged Details from Door with Wall Treatment, Old Renaissance*

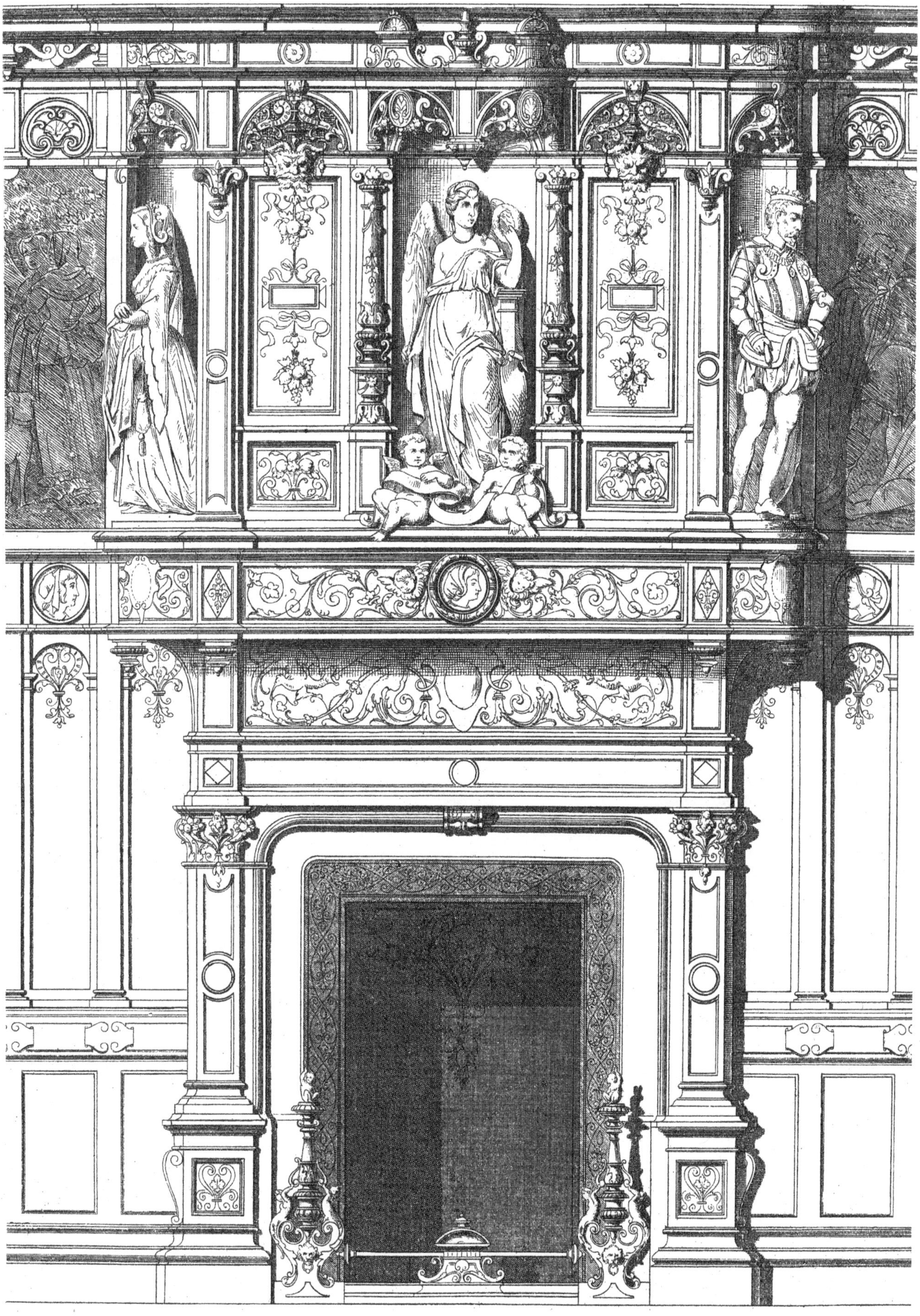

Chimney Piece, Old Renaissance PLATE 31

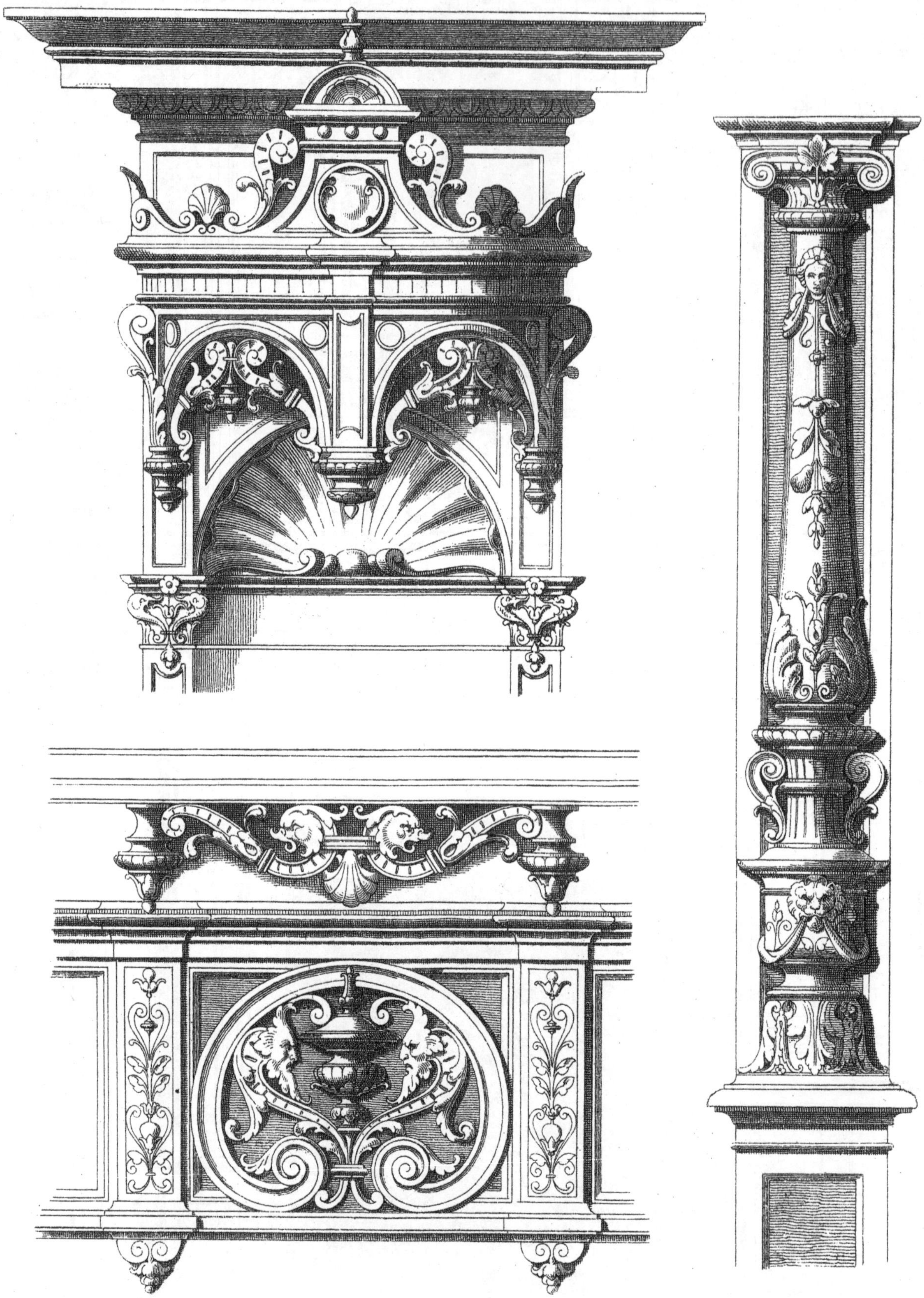

PLATE 32 *Enlarged Details from Chimney Piece, Old Renaissance*

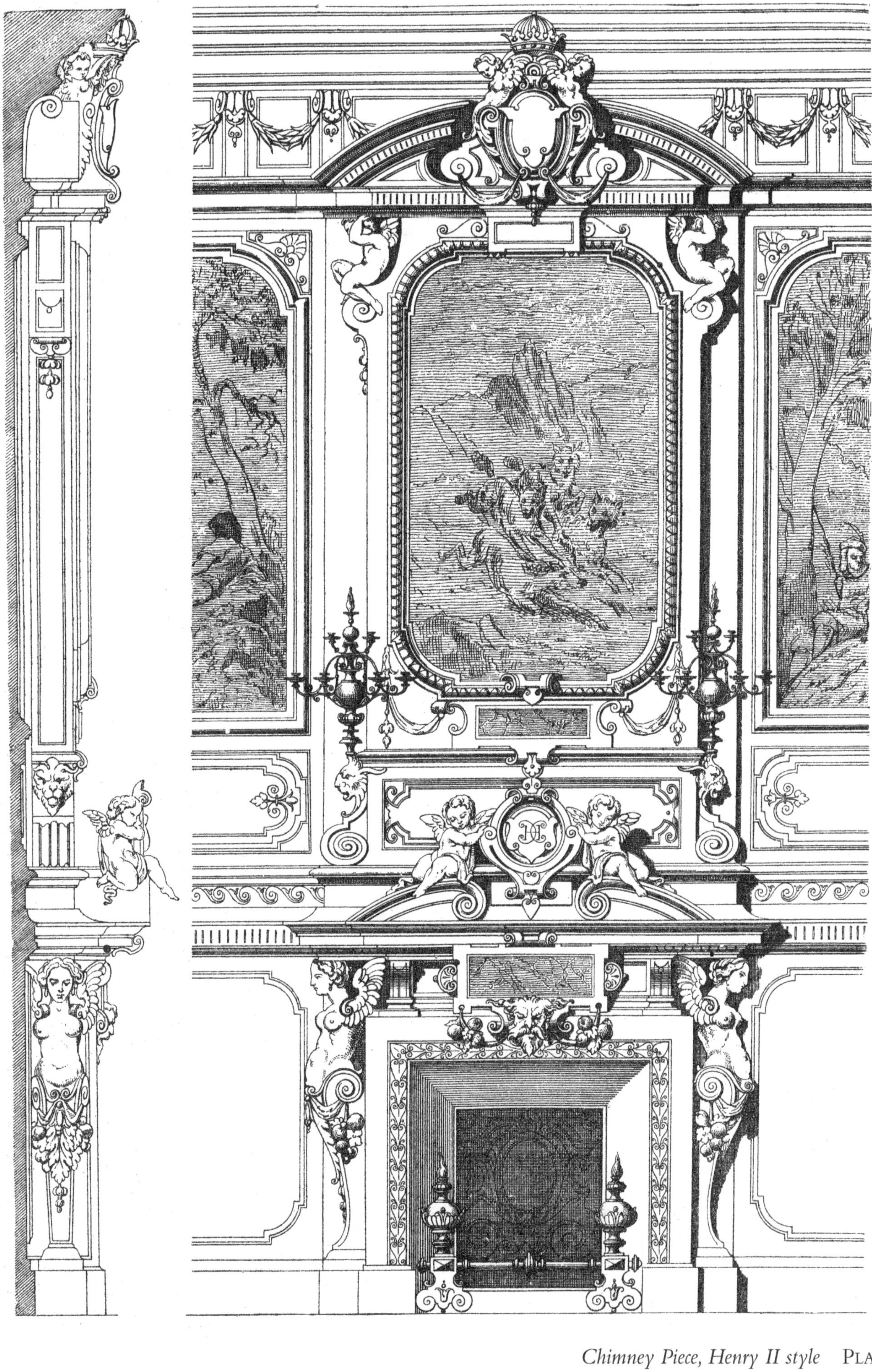

Chimney Piece, Henry II style PLATE 33

PLATE 34 *Designs for Cornices and Crestings*

Dormer in Caen, with Historical Details PLATE 35

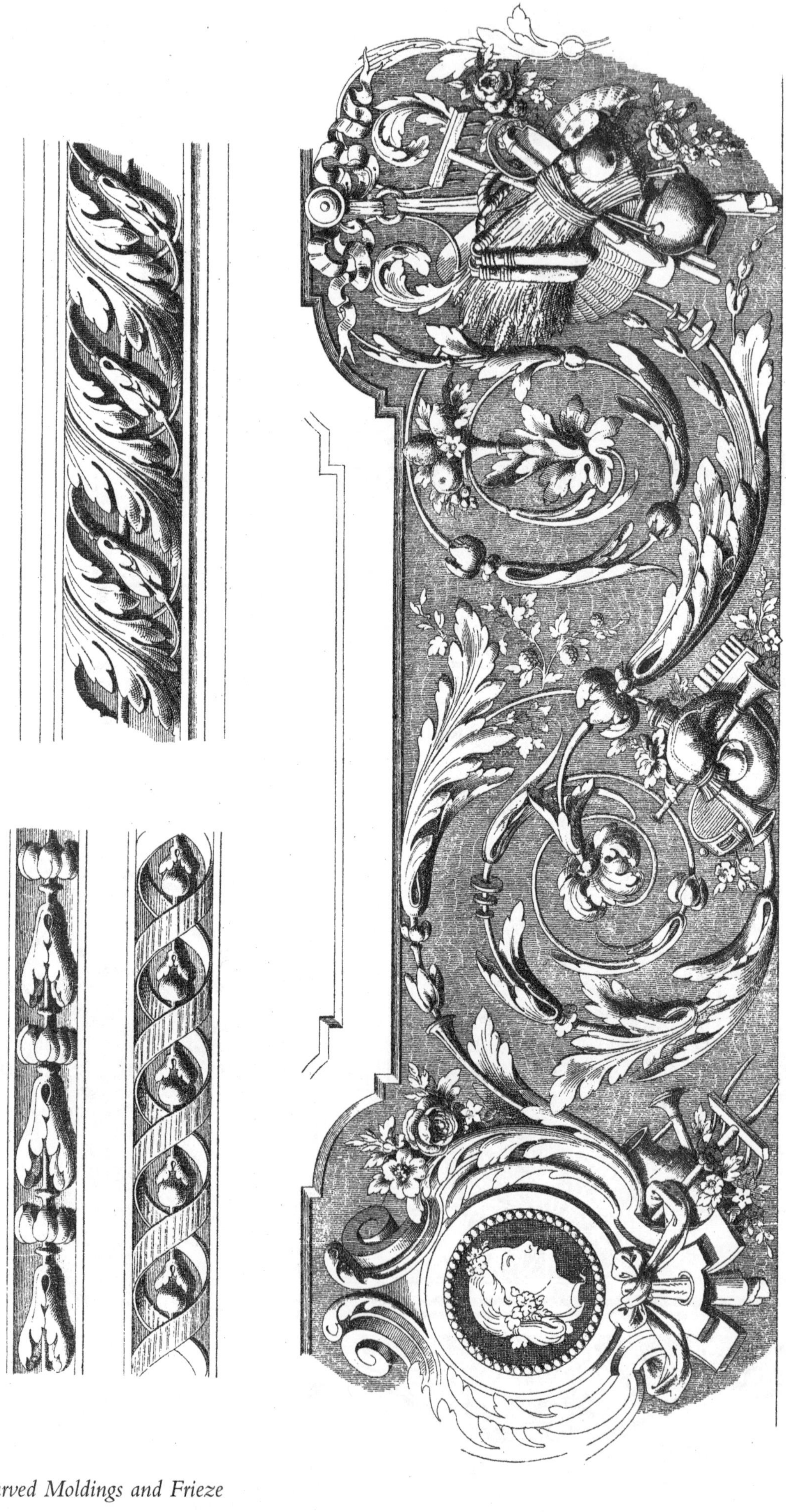

PLATE 36 *Carved Moldings and Frieze*

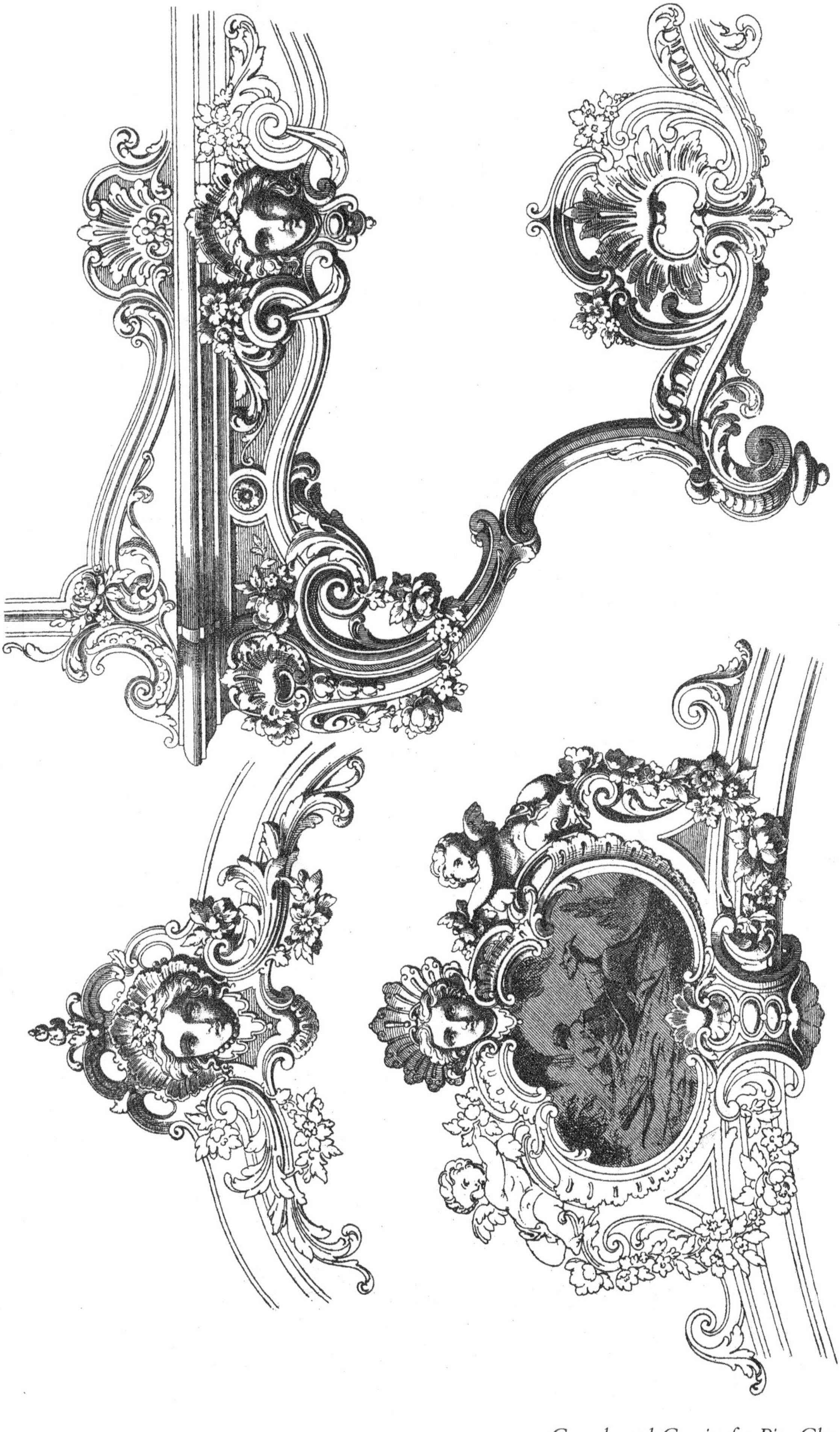

Console and Cornice for Pier Glass PLATE 37

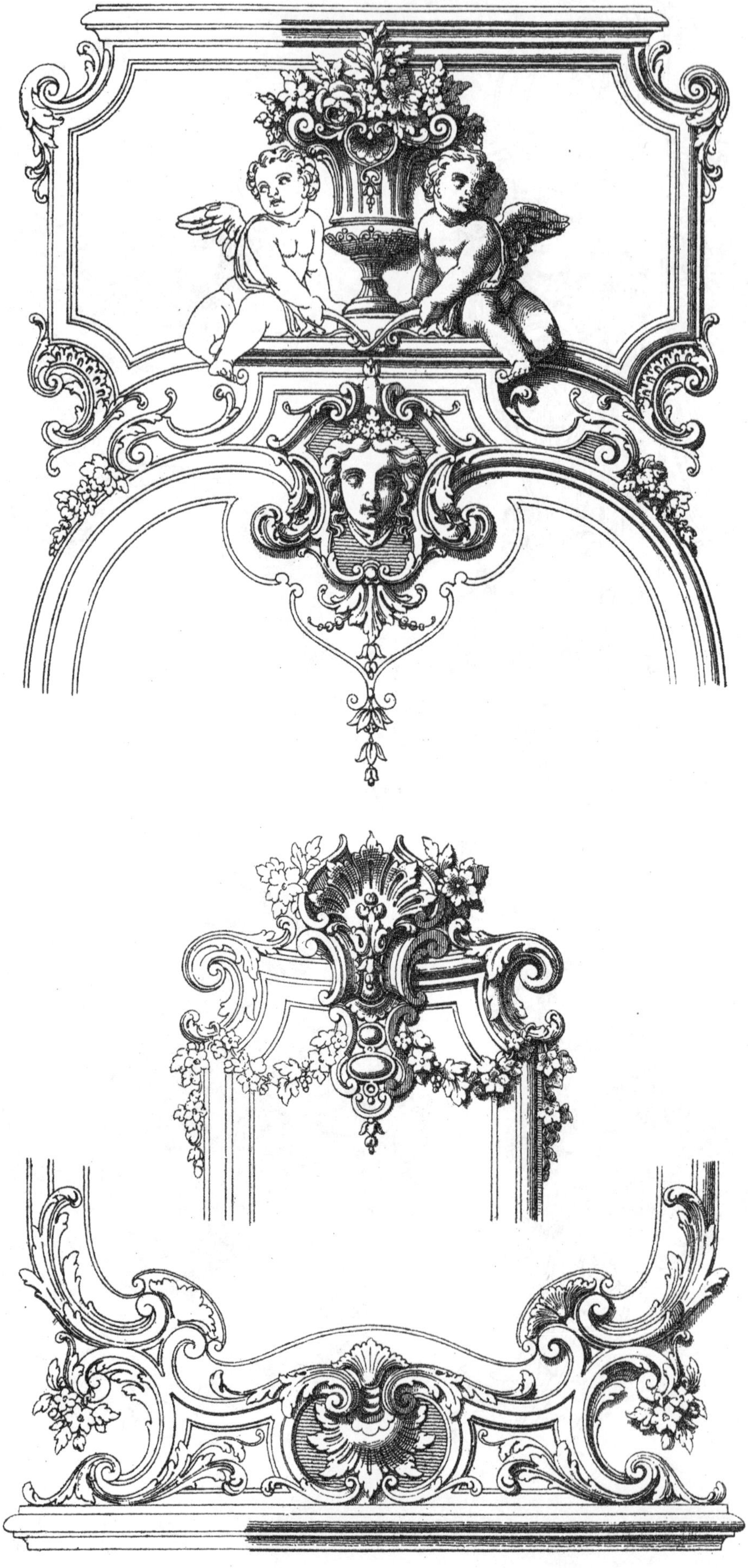

PLATE 38 *Carving of Wainscoting, Louis XV style*

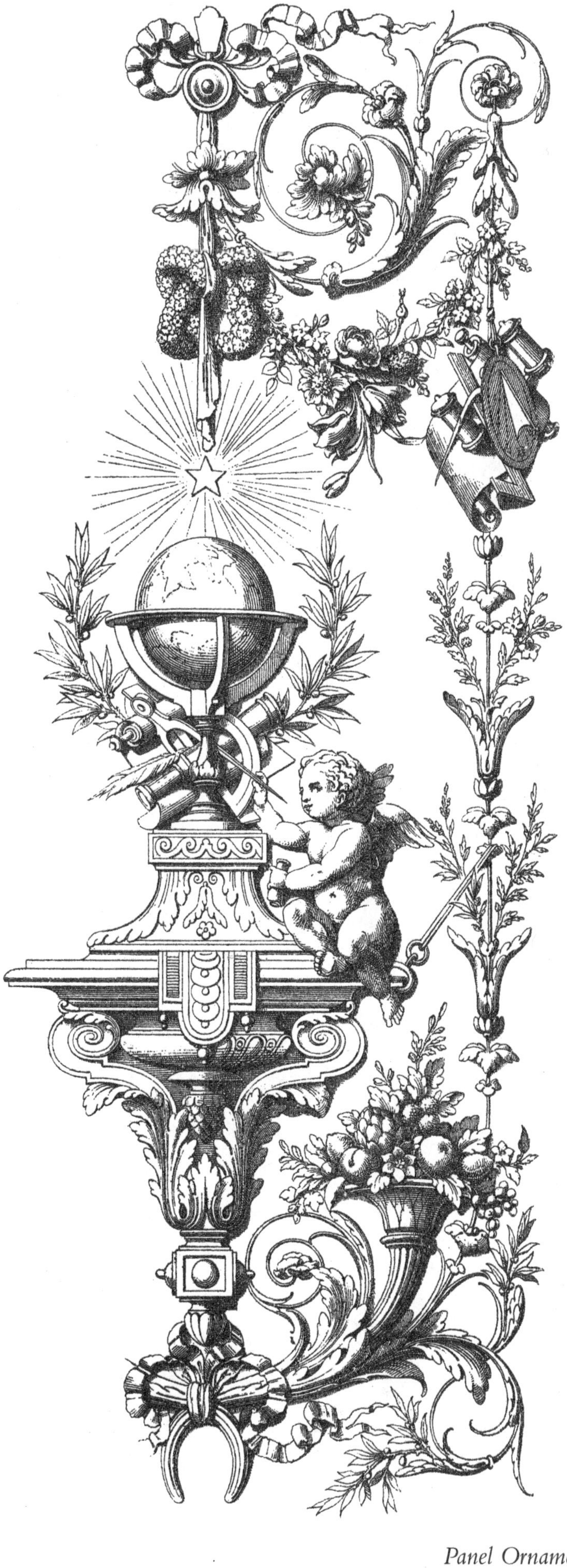

Panel Ornament, Louis XVI style PLATE 39

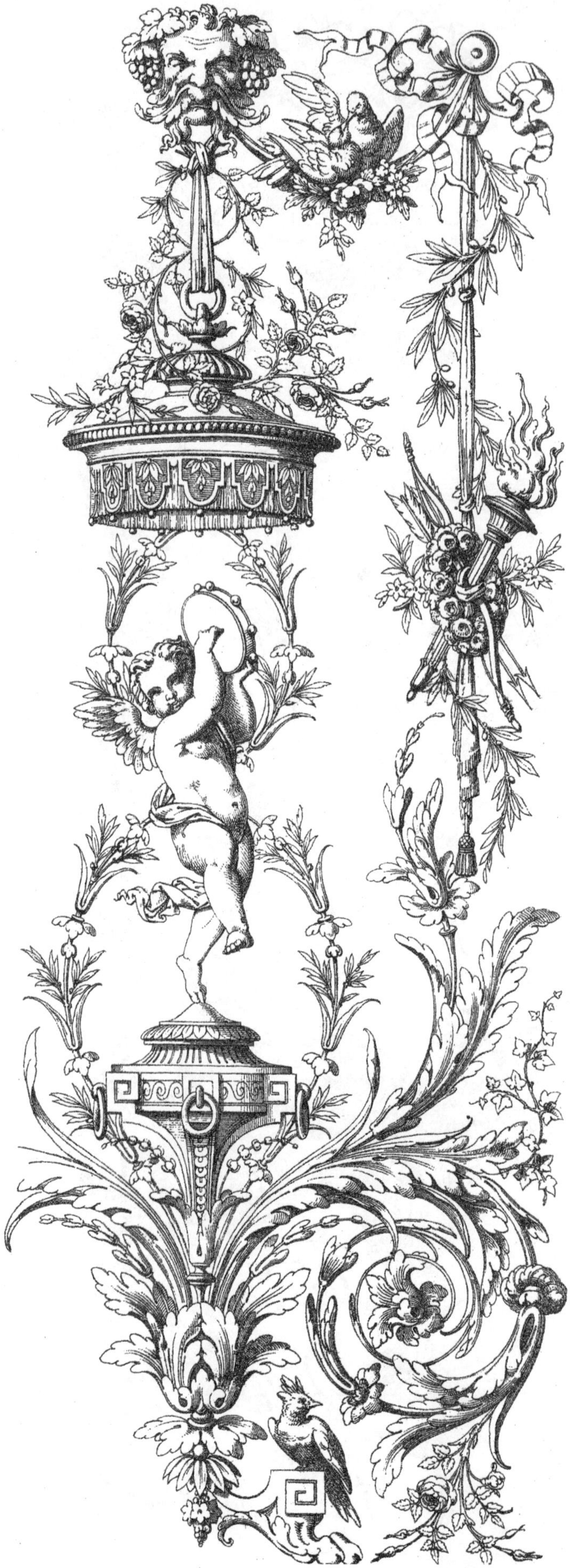

PLATE 40 *Panel Ornament, Louis XVI style*

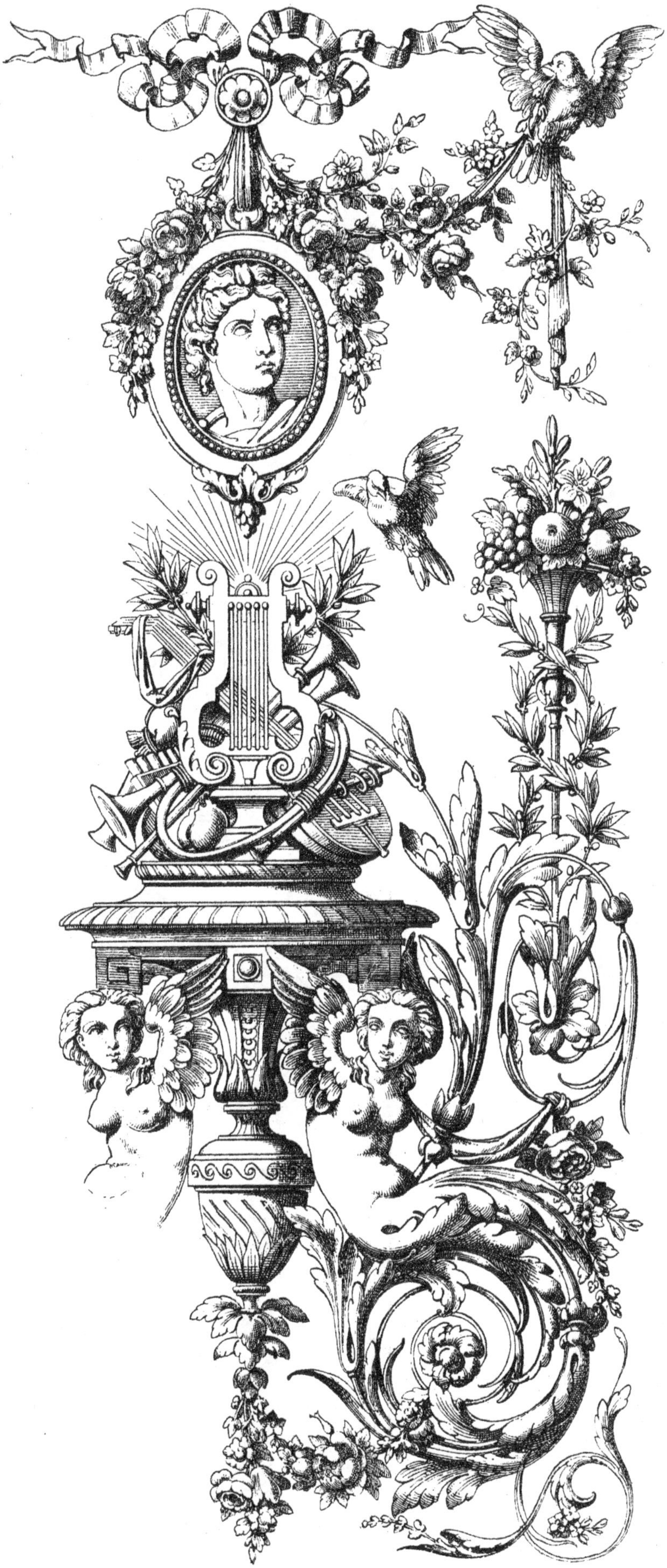

Panel Ornament, Louis XVI style PLATE 41

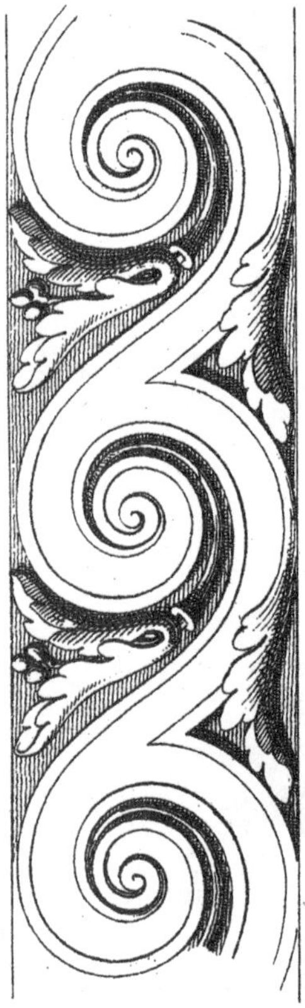

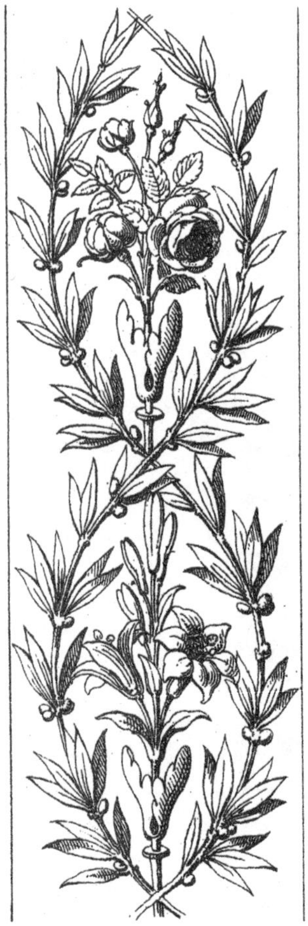

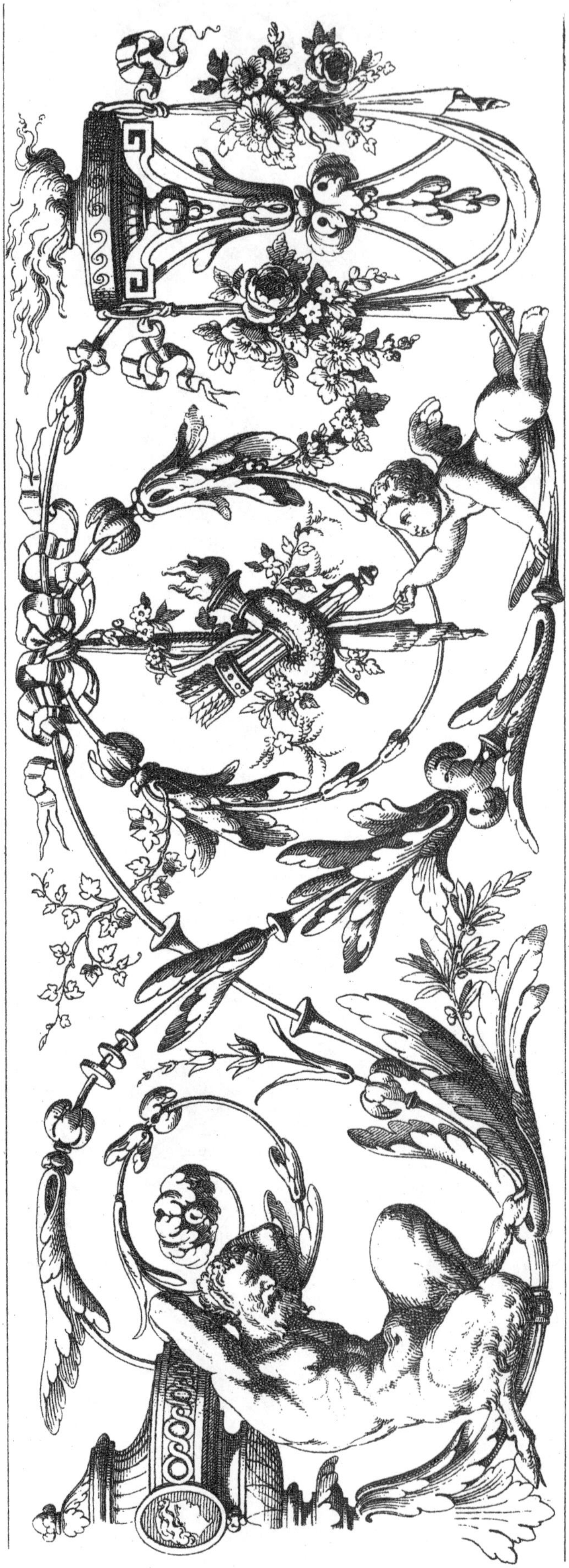

PLATE 42 *Friezes, Louis XVI style*

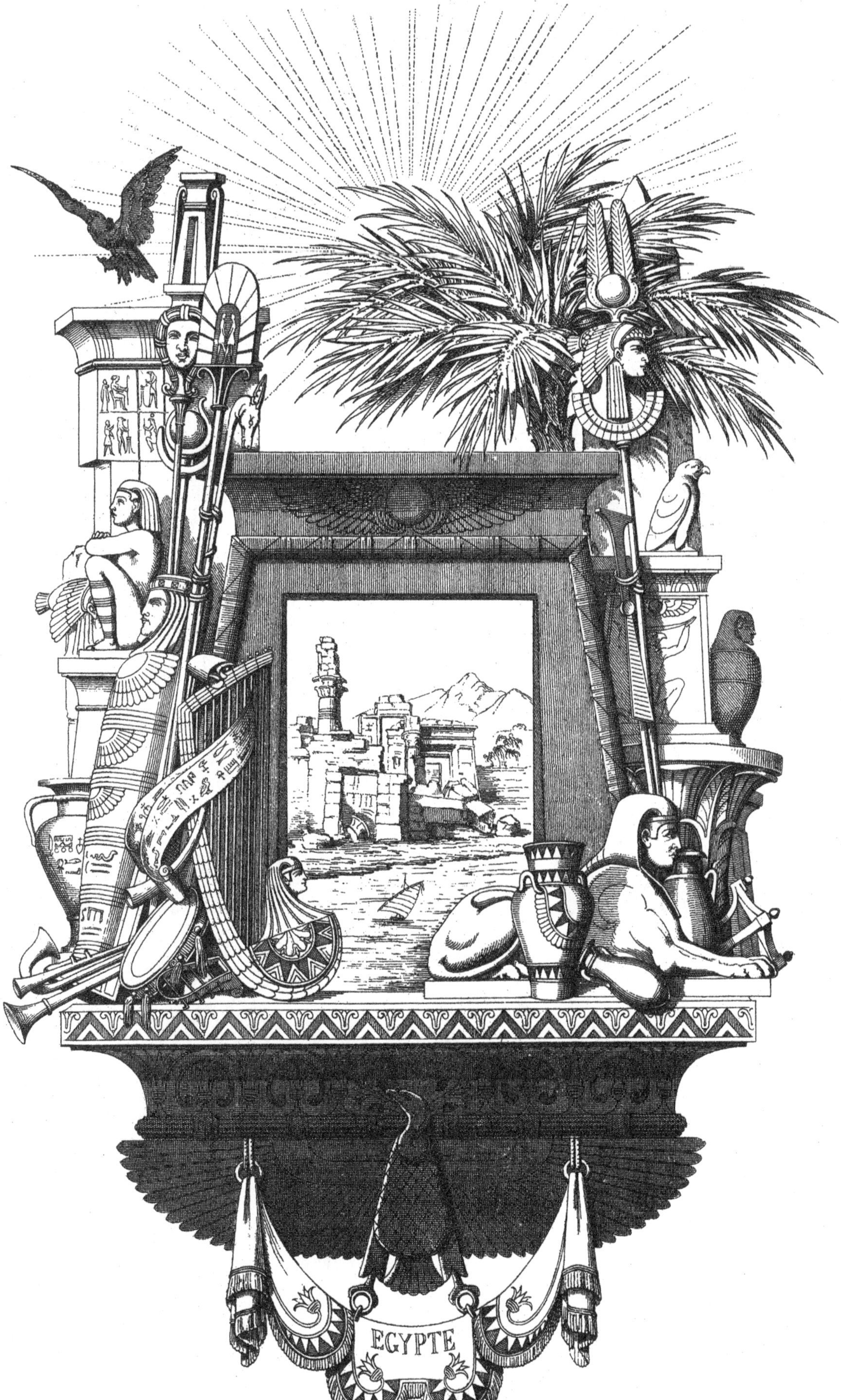

Egyptian Frontispiece, with Historical Details PLATE 43

PLATE 44 *Detail Carving of Wainscoting*

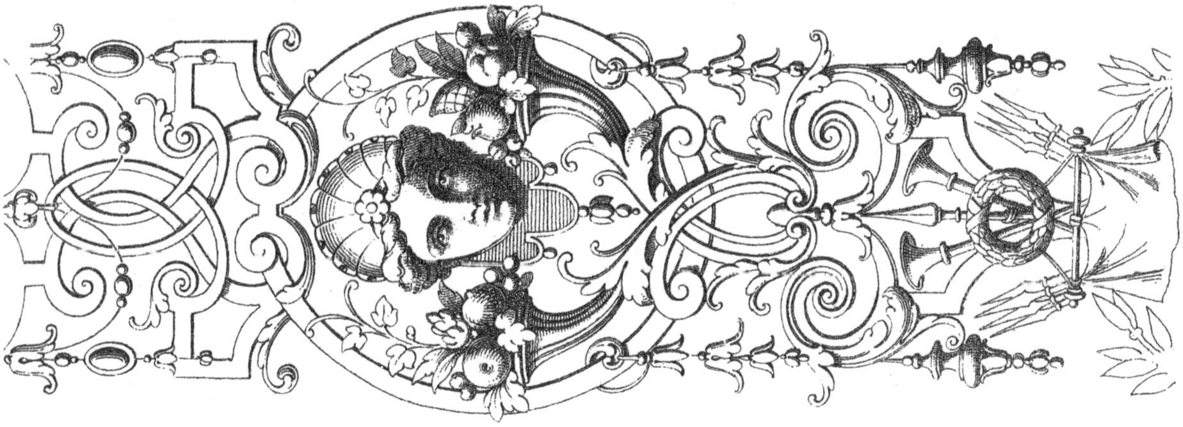

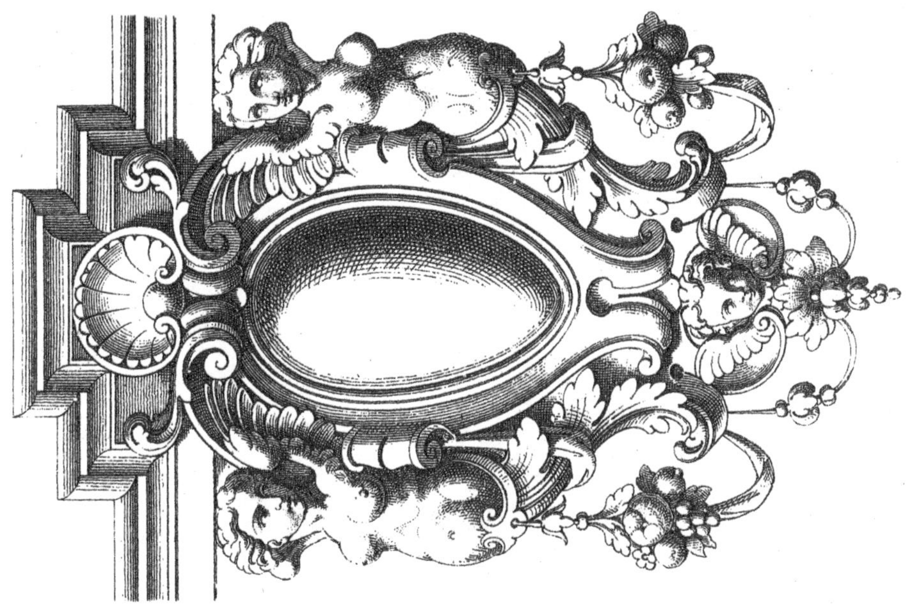

Arabesques and Cartouche PLATE 45

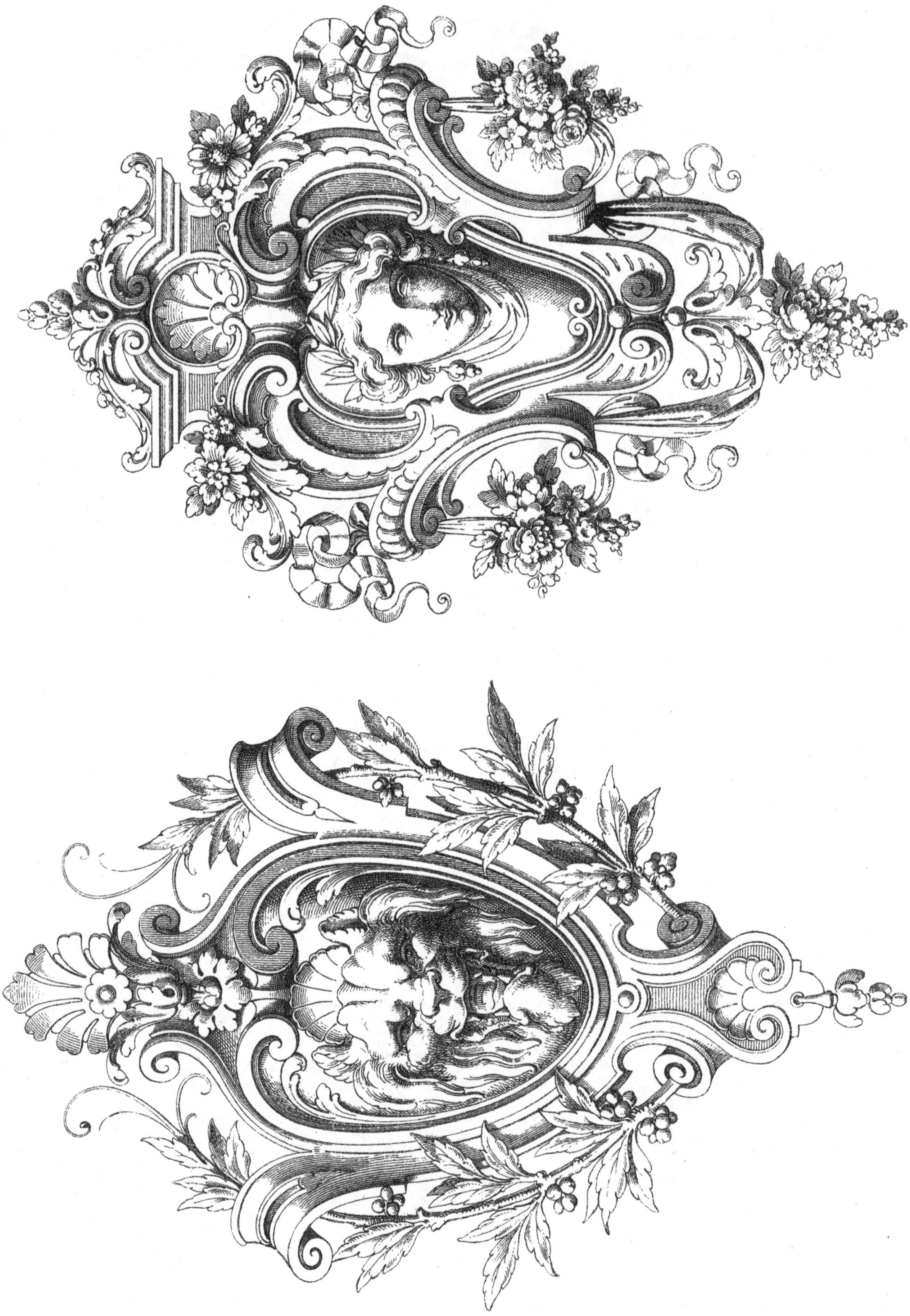

PLATE 46 *Cartouches, Louis XIII style*

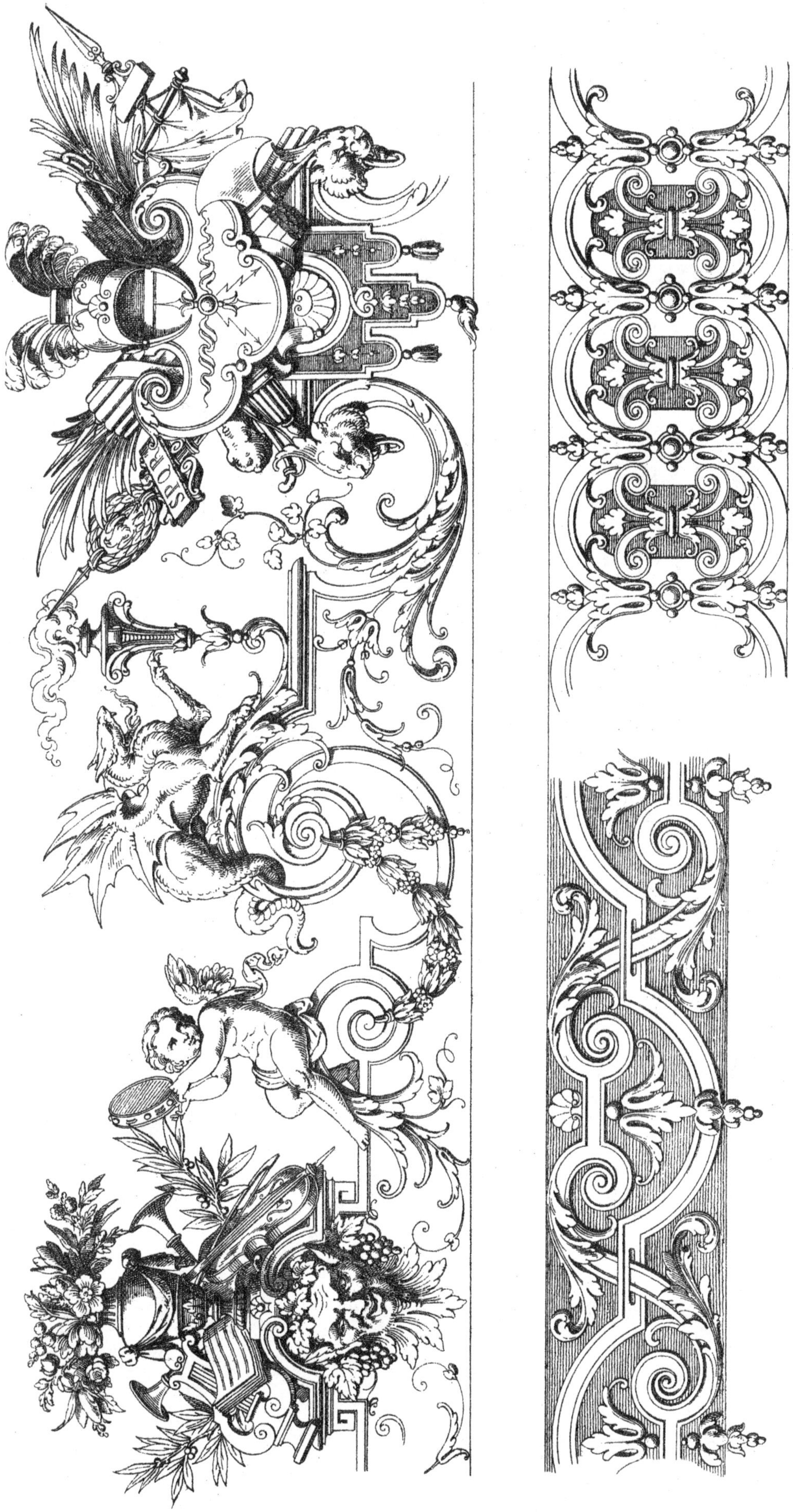

Frieze and Ornamental Bands, Louis XIII style PLATE 47

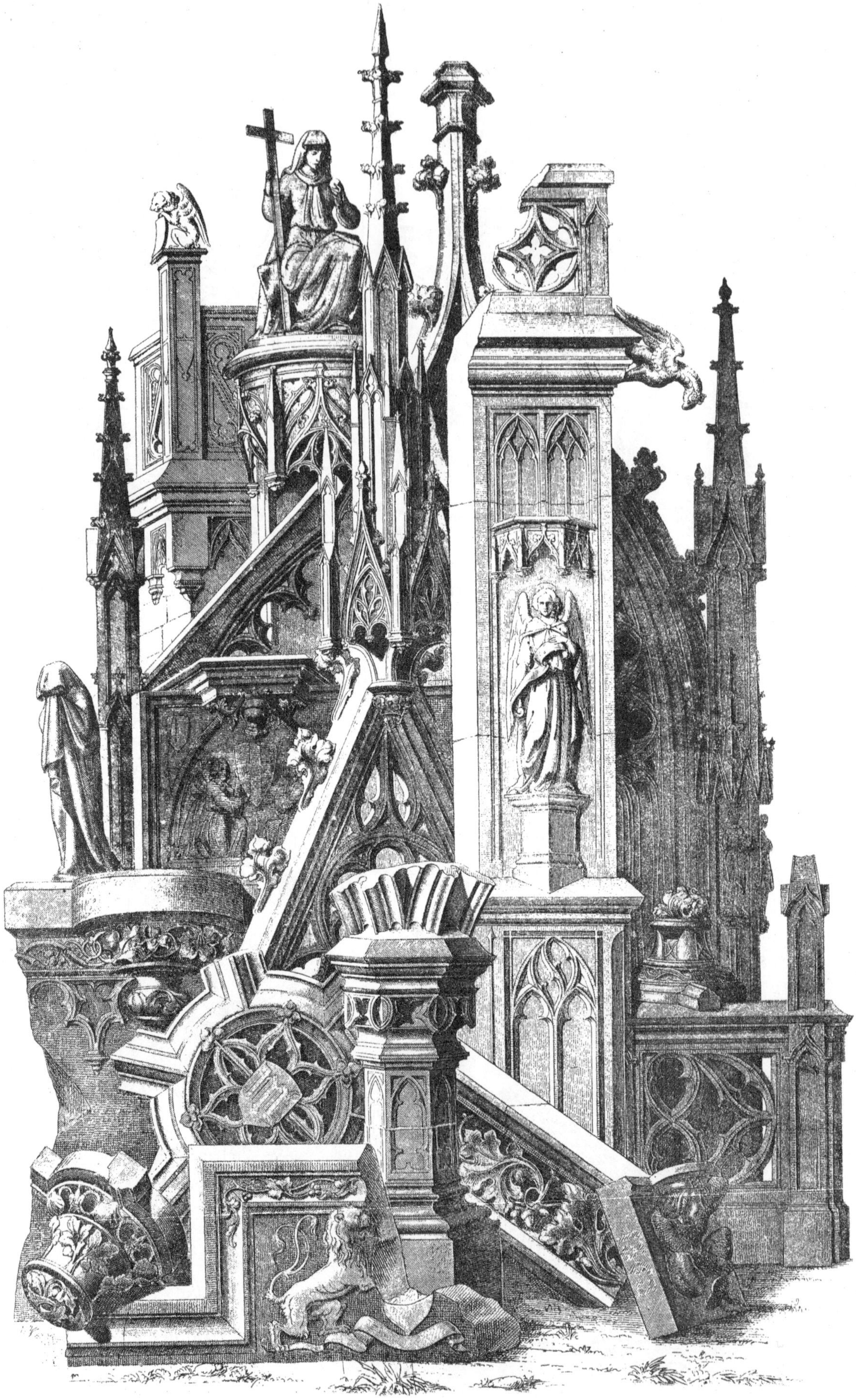

PLATE 48 *Group of Sculpture—fragments from 14th and 15th centuries*

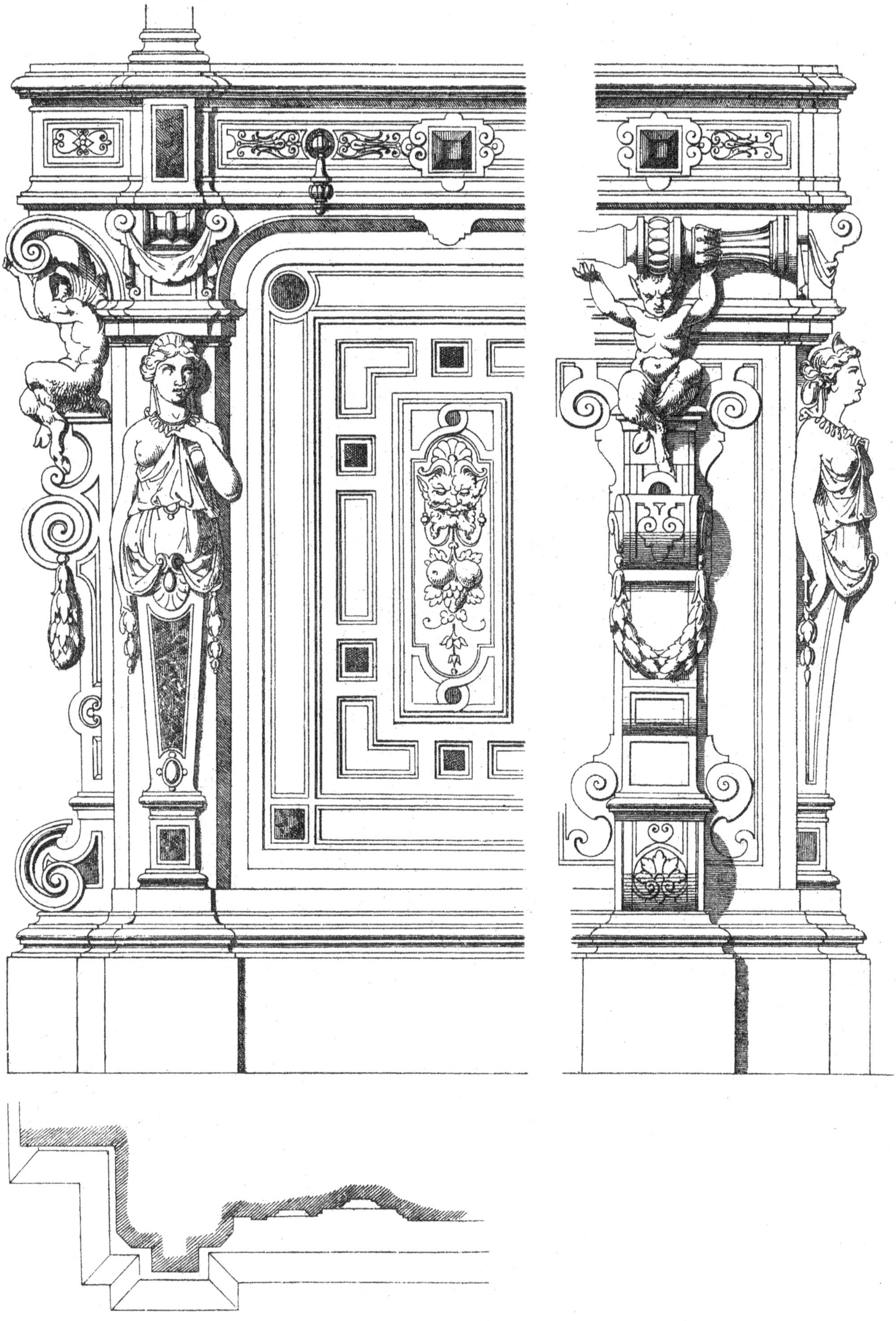

Lower Portion of a Cabinet, Henry II style PLATE 49

PLATE 50 *Mirror Frame and Vase*

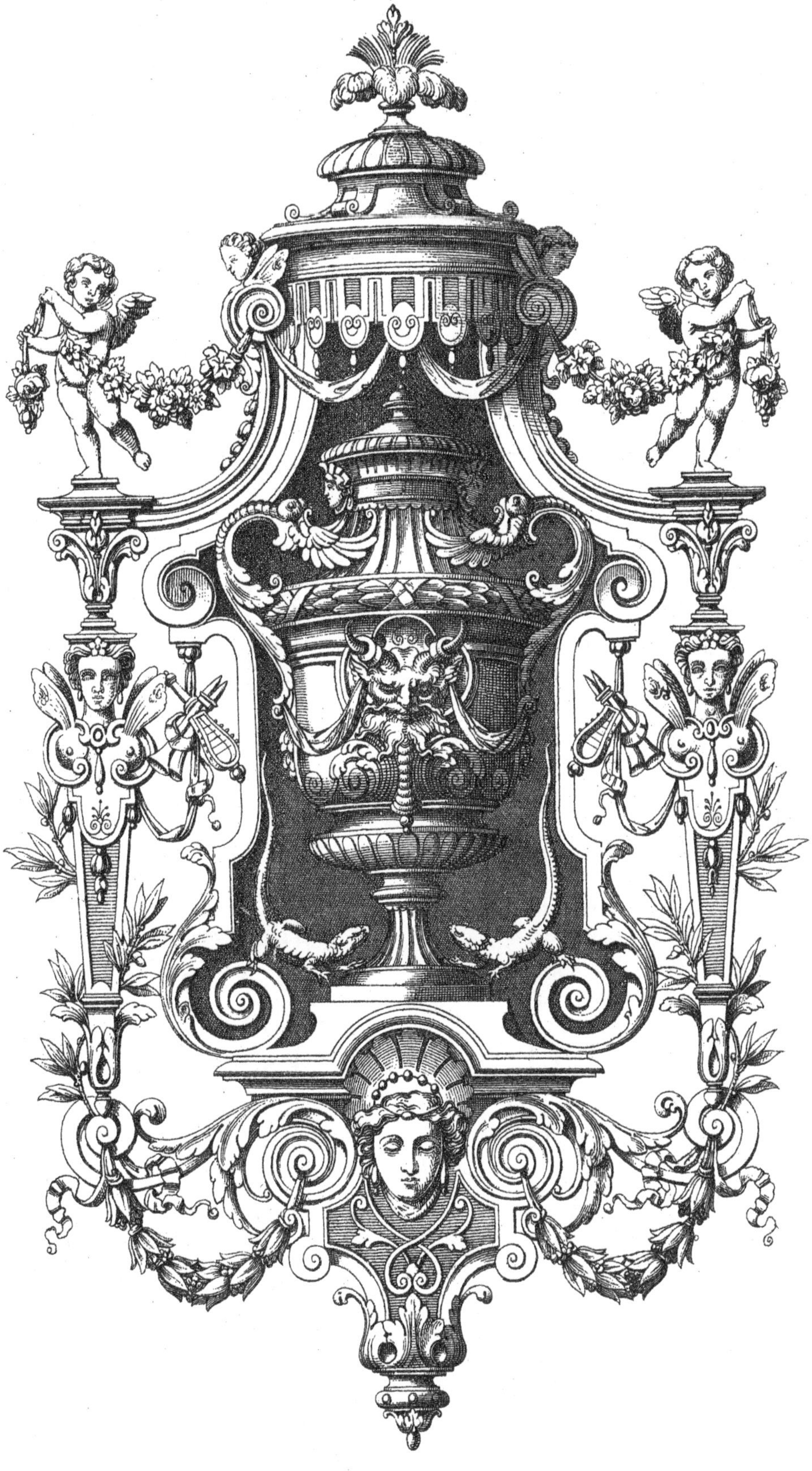

Mirror Frame and Vase PLATE 51

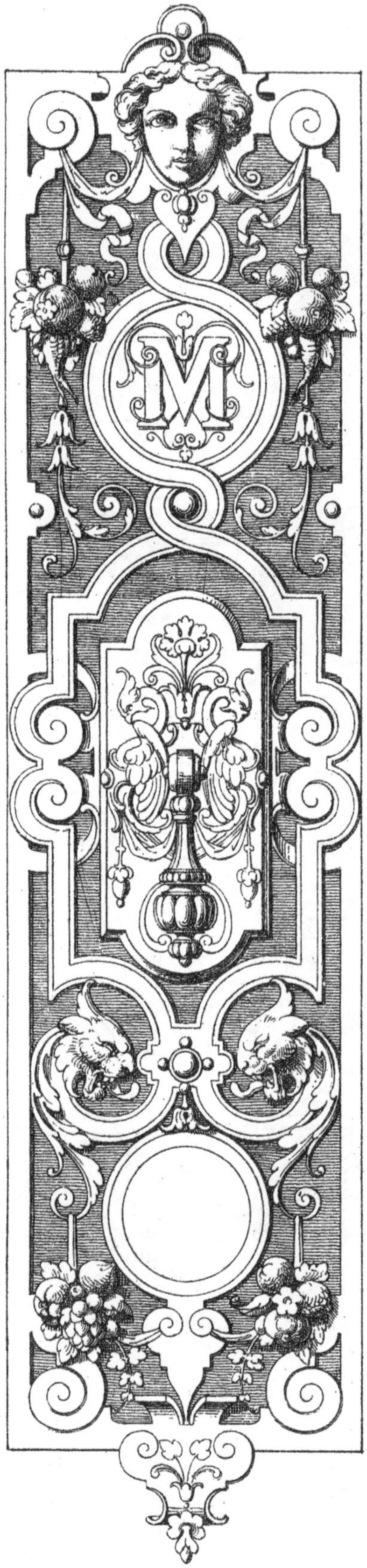

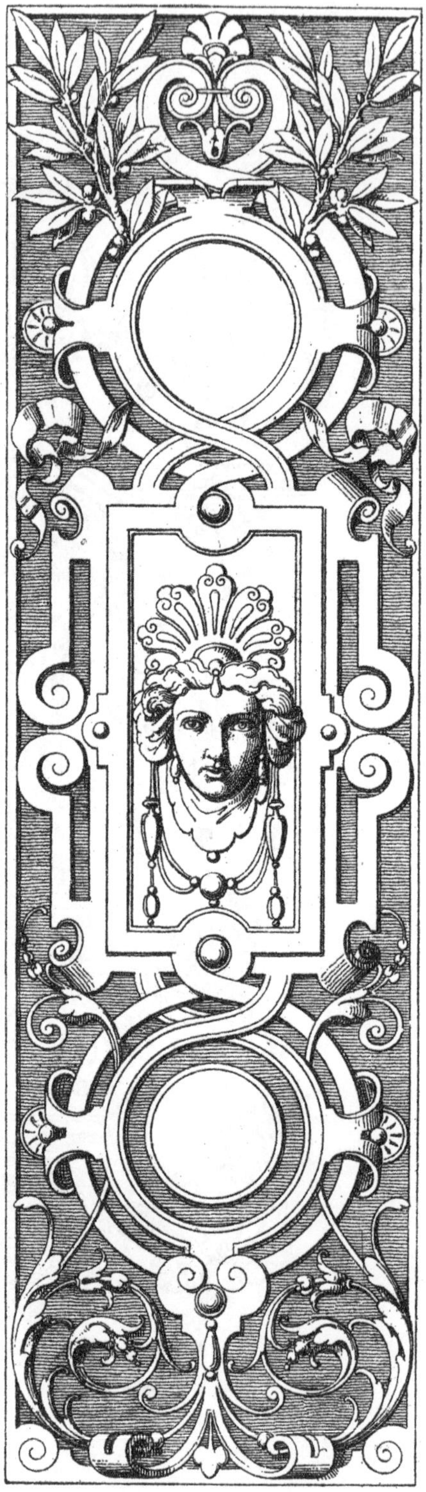

PLATE 52 *Door Panels*

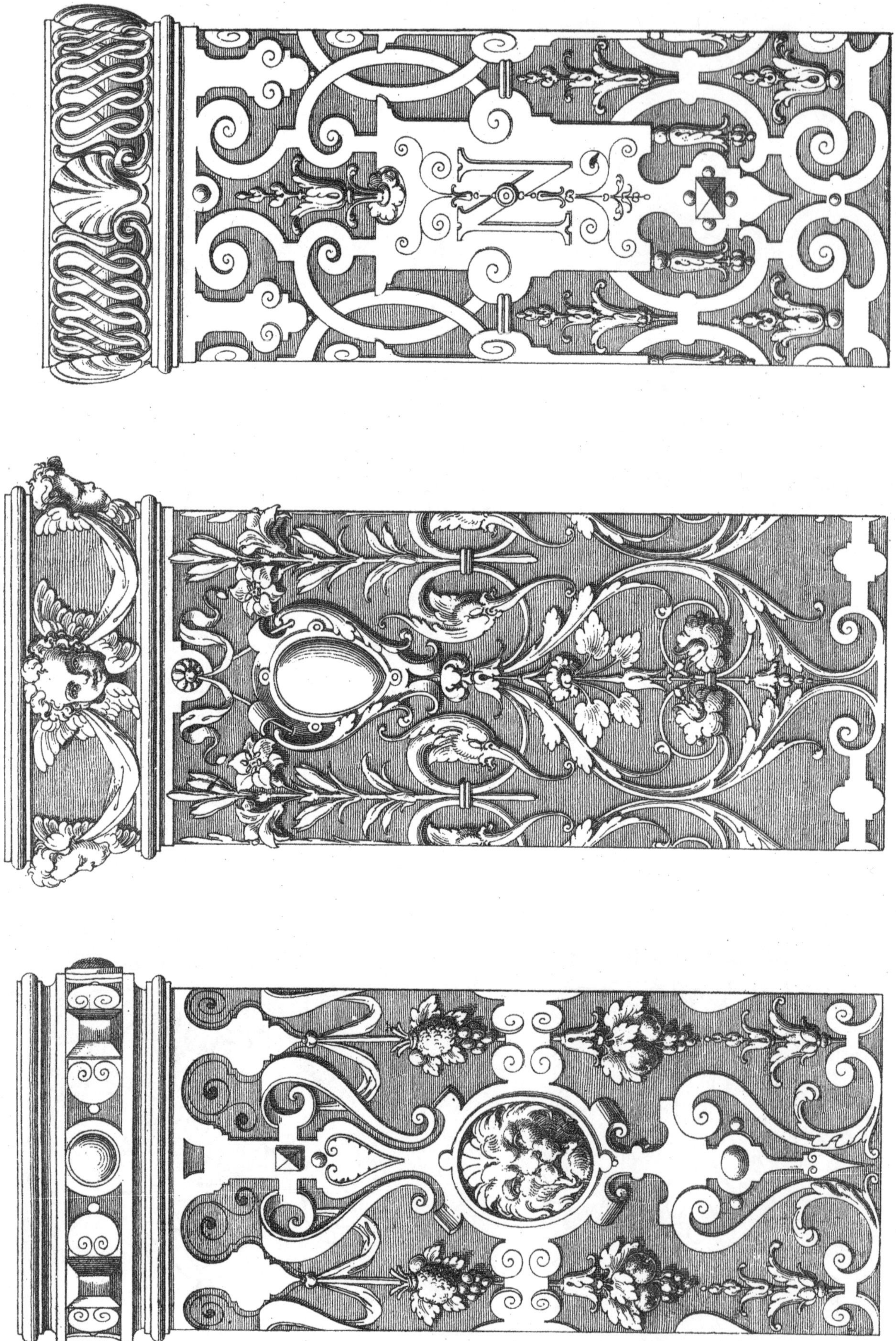

PLATE 54 *Carved Shafts*

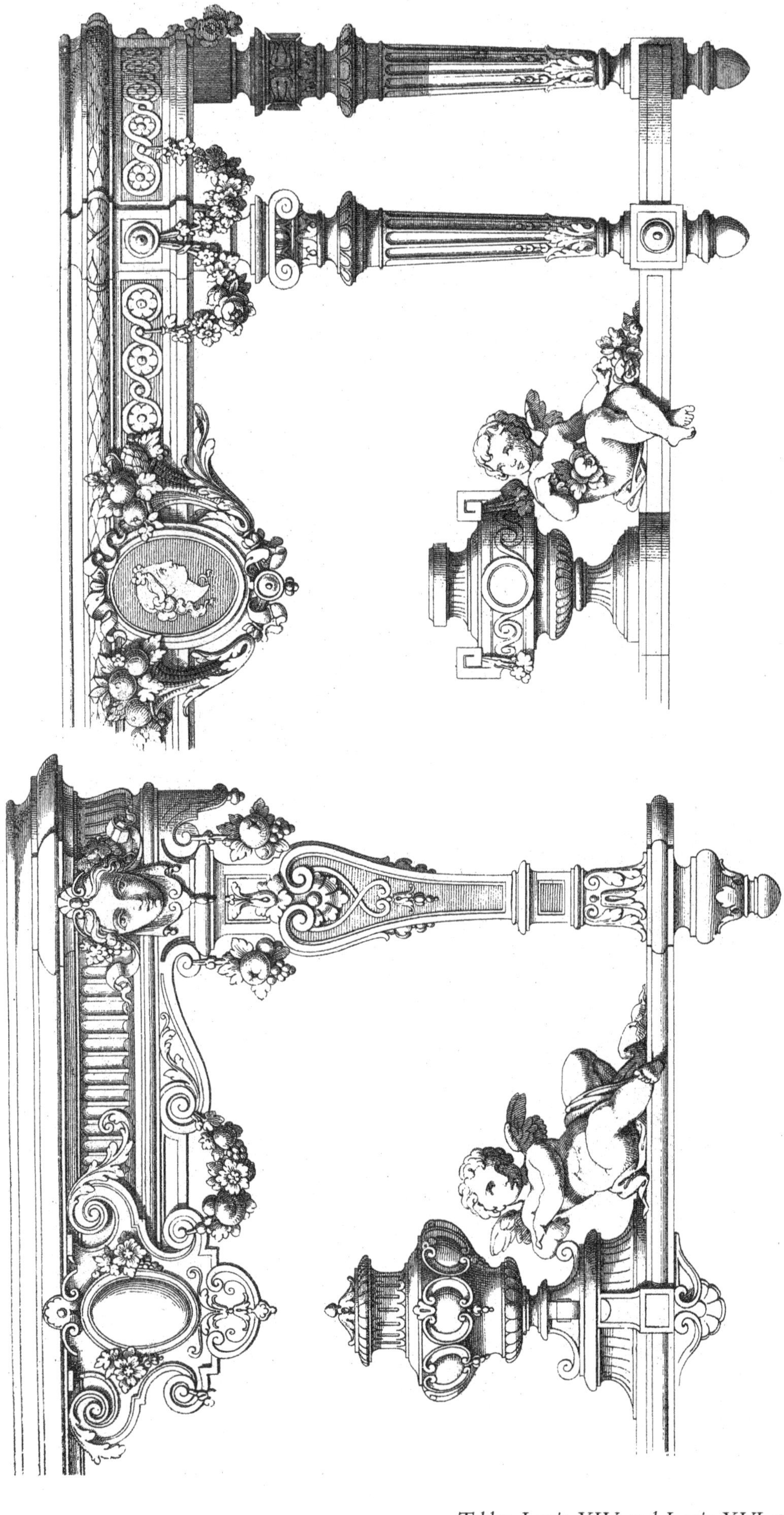

Tables, Louis XIV and Louis XVI style PLATE 55

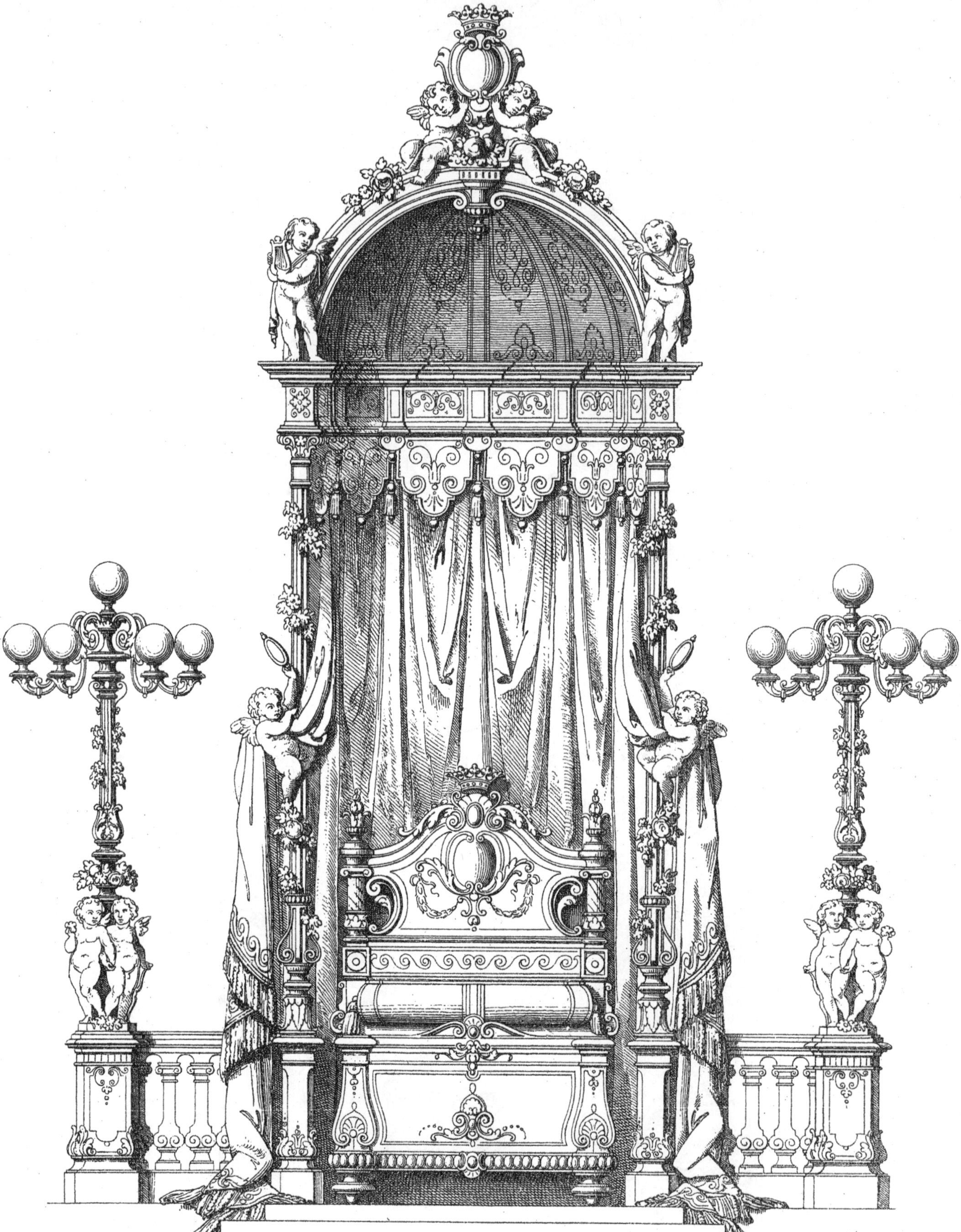

PLATE 56 *Bed of State, Louis XIV style*

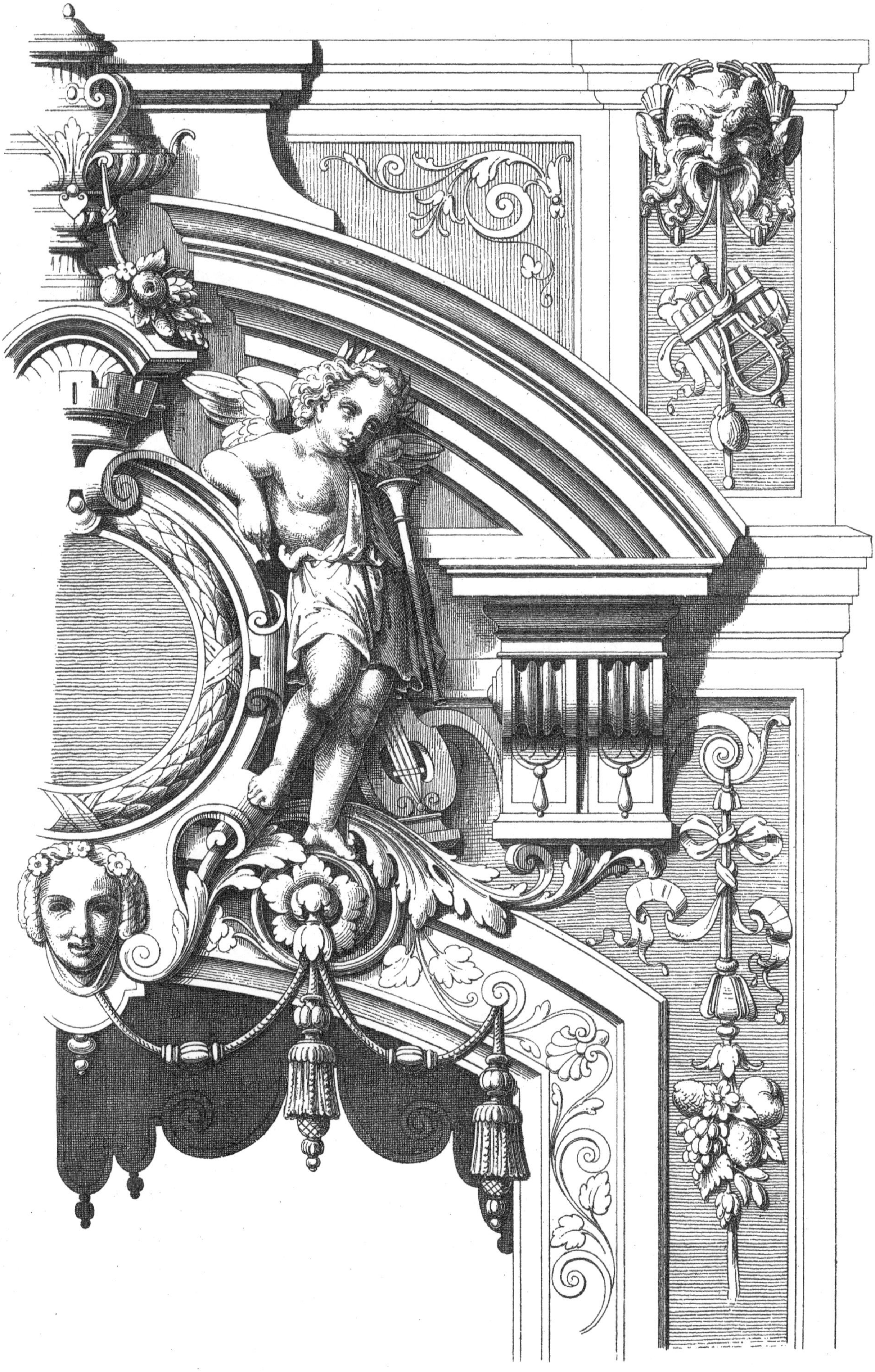

Cornice and Wall Treatment over Proscenium Opera Box PLATE 57

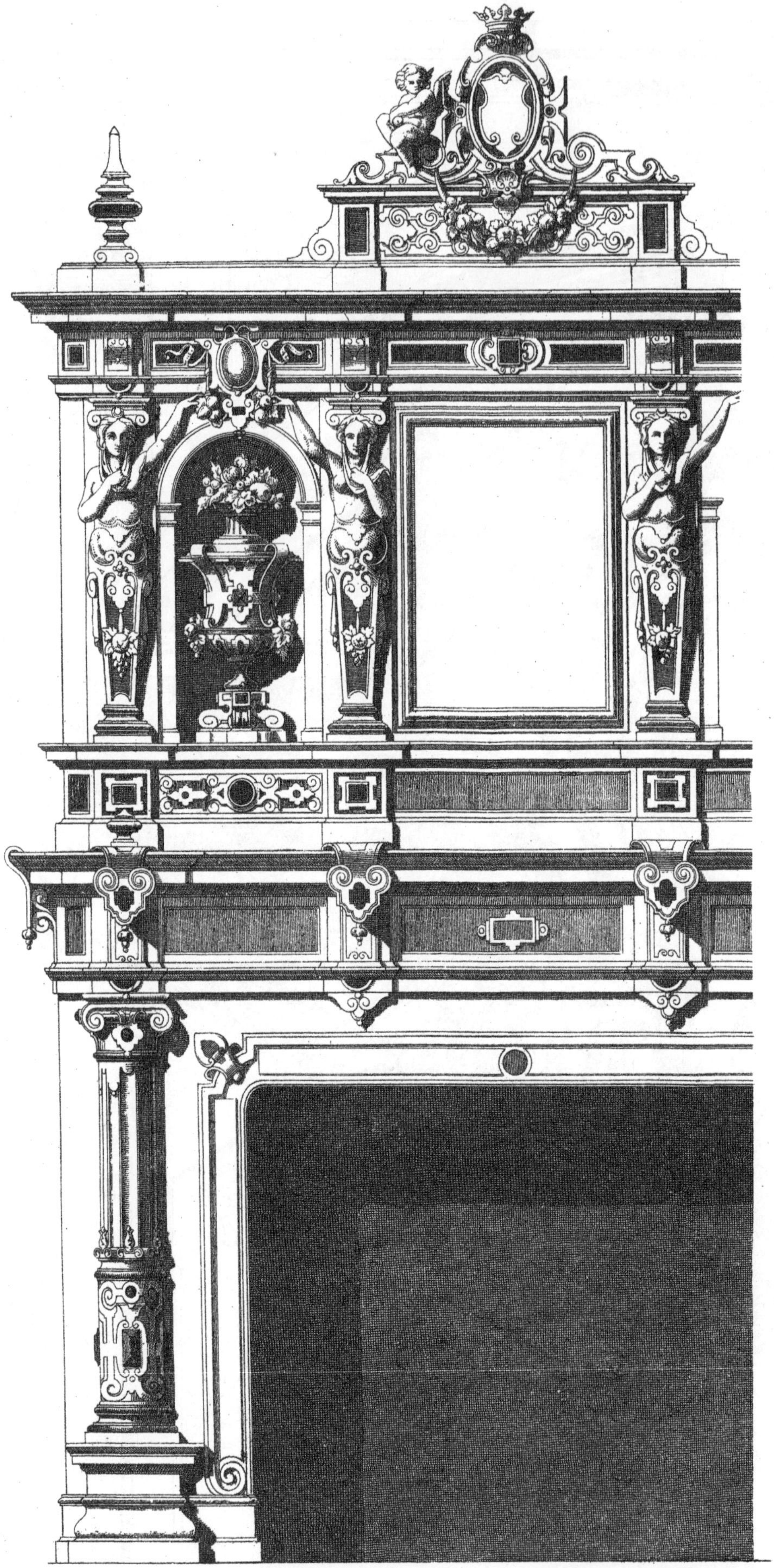

PLATE 58 *Chimney Piece, Elizabethan style*

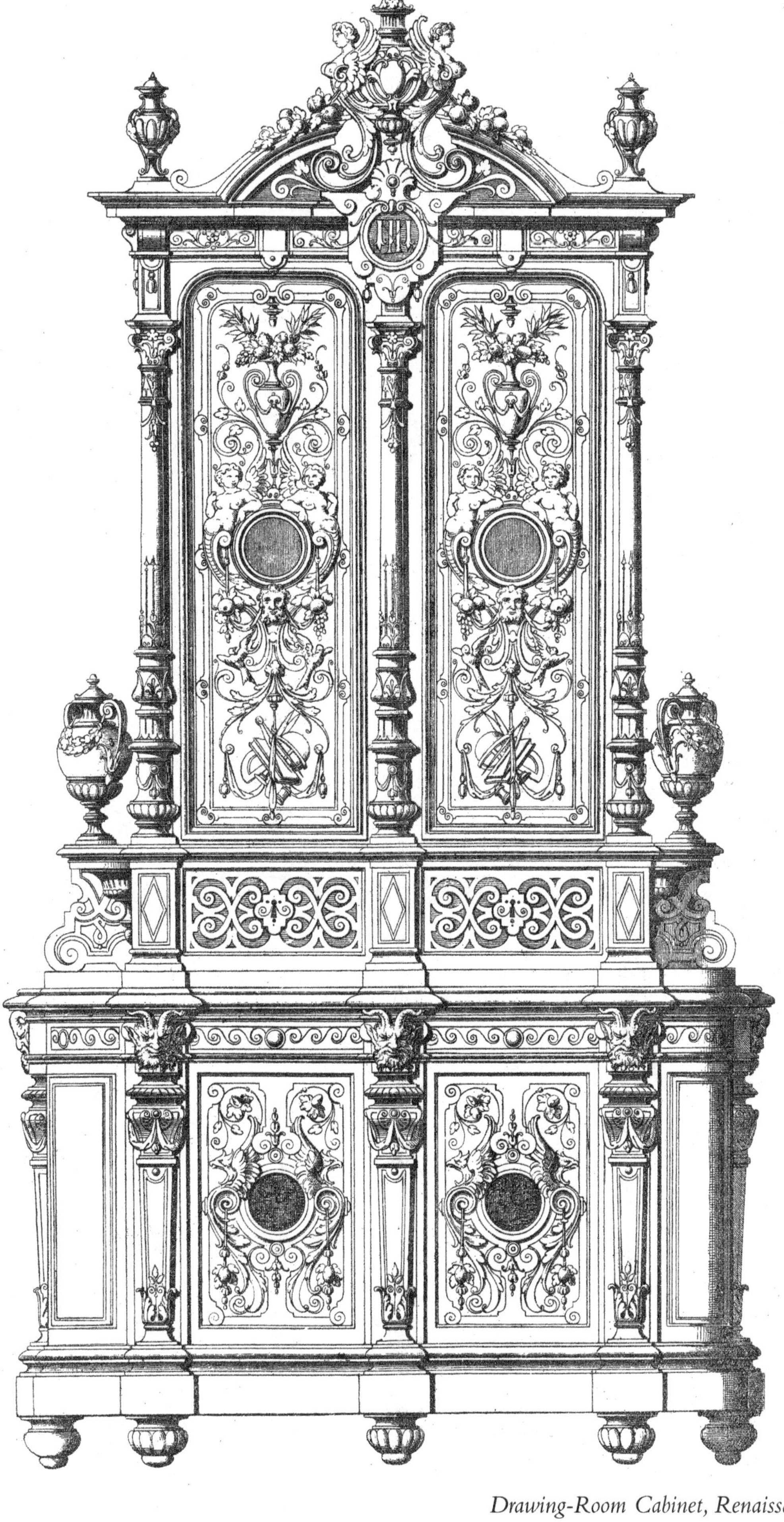

Drawing-Room Cabinet, Renaissance PLATE 59

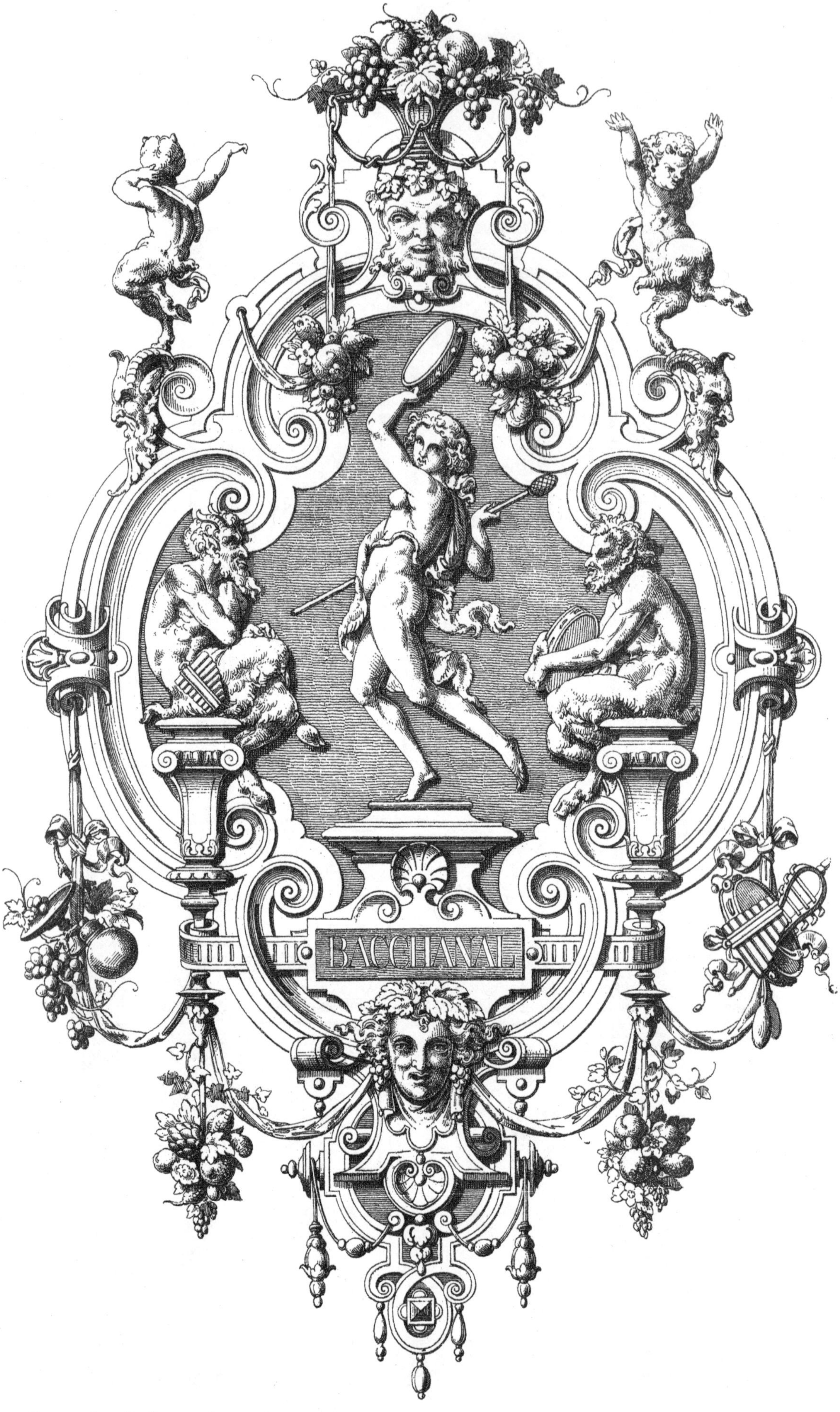

PLATE 60 *Cartouches, Italian style*

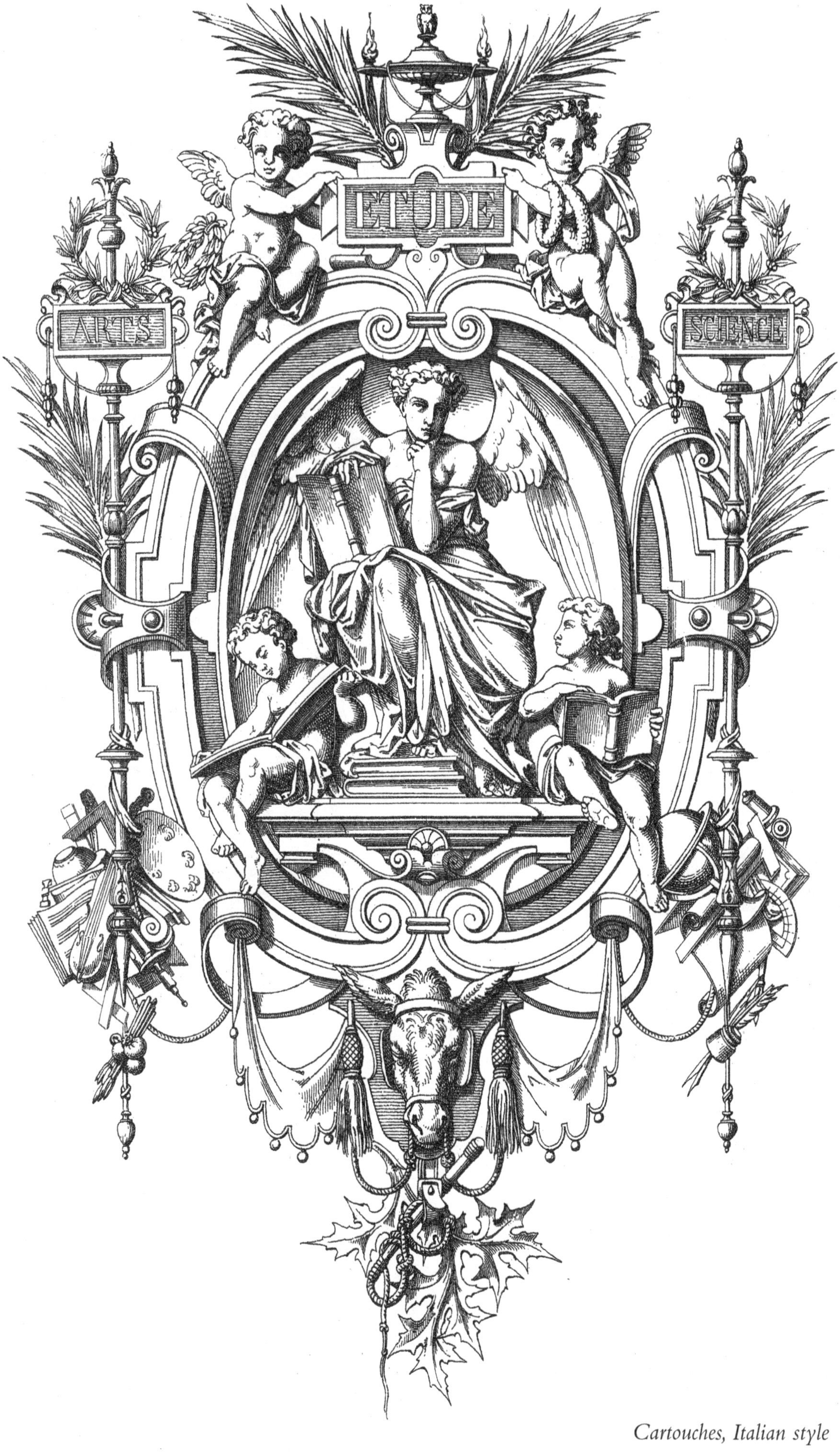
ETUDE
ARTS
SCIENCE

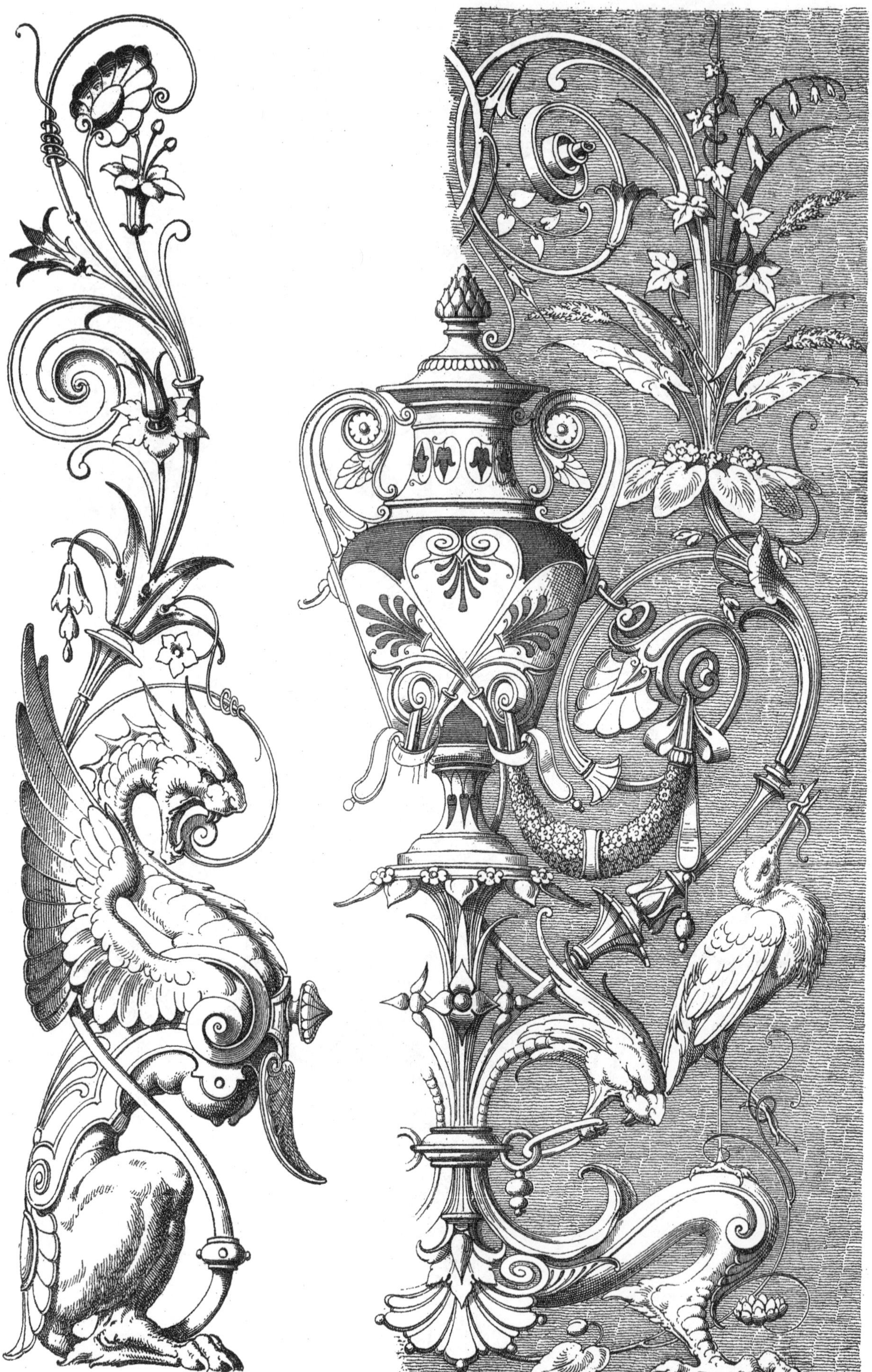

PLATE 62 *Arabesques*